GERARD MANLEY HOPKINS

A Study of His Ignatian Spirit

GERARD MANLEY HOPKINS

A Study of His Ignatian Spirit

by

David A. Downes

BOOKMAN ASSOCIATES

New York 3

TO: DAVID MICHAEL and URSULA JULIA DOWNES
      with affection and gratitude;

TO: AUDREY with love.

Contents

Contents

Introduction

Historians of religion have noted that, beginning in the twelfth century and continuing to the seventeenth century, there developed a tradition of meditative prayer. This form of prayer as it evolved through the centuries tended to become more and more methodical until a time came when one could talk about methods of mental prayer. Until the seventeenth century, however, there was no one meditative method which one might classify as universal, though some systems were better known and more often used. In the sixteenth century (1521-41), St. Ignatius Loyola composed a series of meditative exercises called *The Spiritual Exercises*. These became the fundamental instrument of mental prayer for the religious order which he founded, the Society of Jesus. Because of the remarkable success of the Society during the years which we know as the Counter-Reformation, these Exercises became well known throughout all of Europe.

It was not only, however, because they were well known that they had so remarkable an influence on mental prayer; it was also because St. Ignatius' Exercises were really a synthesis and summation of the whole early tradition of meditation. They represent the emergence of an exact and universal method of meditative and contemplative prayer, a culmination of four centuries of effort. Moreover, to this very day, no other method has supplanted them. Their manner and matter form the basis in some measure of all subsequent methods of meditation.[1]

Professor Louis L. Martz, in a fine study,[2] suggests that this spirit of meditation fostered a tradition of religious poetry which had as its first important example, Robert Southwell, and reached its height in the poetry of the Metaphysical Poets and Milton. During the eighteenth century and into the nineteenth century this tradition is less perceptible, though it can be found in the poetry of Blake and Wordsworth; it is particularly evident in the poetry of Parnell, Blair, and Young, better known as the "Graveyard School." He further suggests

9

that in the latter half of the nineteenth century there emerged a new energy within the meditative tradition in the poetry of Hopkins, who is seen "as the forerunner of a new era of meditative poetry, represented in the later poetry of Yeats and Eliot, and found also in portions of the work of Allen Tate, Richard Eberhart, Dylan Thomas and Robert Lowell."[3]

Accepting this delineation of a tradition of meditative poetry, this book is a reading of G. M. Hopkins as a meditative poet whose poetic experience originated primarily from his learning and living the *Spiritual Exercises* of St. Ignatius Loyola. It is the main intent of this study to examine to what extent Hopkins' art was influenced by Ignatian spirituality. Therefore, those poems and papers written after he became a Jesuit make up the prime evidence. Especially important is a set of notes, just now fully published, which Hopkins wrote for a projected commentary on the Spiritual Exercises. They offer important guides regarding the esthetic, philosophical, and theological implications that the Exercises had for the poet.

I have taken note of other scholars and critics of Hopkins wherever they seemed to be helpful. Chief among these are W. H. Gardner whose edition of Hopkins' poetry is definitive and whose two-volume work still remains the most exhaustive study; Humphry House, the first editor of the journals and papers, whose work has been ably completed by Mr. Graham Storey; John Pick who has written the best introduction to Hopkins; Christopher Devlin, S.J., who has done the best scholarship on Hopkins and Scotus, and has recently done a very scholarly job of editing Hopkins' spiritual writings; D. A. Bischoff, S.J., who, in writing Hopkins' biography, has amassed the fullest evidence on the life of the poet; W. A. M. Peters, S.J., whose essay penetrates a difficult poetic technique; and recently, Alan Heuser, whose cryptic study opens up the influences of Pre-Raphaelite sensationalism and Greek philosophy on Hopkins' vision.

Since there are early poems and papers which have much in common with the spirit of the founder of the Society of Jesus, I have called attention to this fact to further support my contention regarding the correlation between the Ignatian spirit and the spirit that pervades Hopkins' art. This latter evidence is admittedly of a secondary nature, but it is important because it shows how well suited Hopkins' religious proclivities were for the sort of conversion they were to undergo by his becoming a Catholic and especially a Jesuit. Some of the religious attitudes he held as a Jesuit, and expressed in his poems of the Jesuit period, he held and wrote of as an Anglican. His conversion was the turning point in his life, and no doubt it was a profound change; but the movement toward that conversion can be seen in his early notebooks and his early poems.

In preparing this study, it occurred to me that many a professional as well as average reader may have had little contact with the *Spiritual Exercises of St. Ignatius.* Moreover, the Exercises themselves cannot be fully understood just by reading them. Commentators must be consulted. Therefore, to be able to appreciate the structure of the Ignatian meditation and its content, to discern the peculiar spirit which is called Ignatian, I urge such readers to consult one or more of the reputable commentaries on the Spiritual Exercises. H. Bremond, J. P. Calveras, Jean Danielou, I. Iparraguirre, H. Pinard De La Boullaye, P. Pourrat, and Hugo Rahner have written excellent guides to Ignatian spirituality.[4] Their writings are illuminating, perceptive, and fruitful. This study presumes a more than general familiarity with the form and content of the Spiritual Exercises as well as a rather accurate concept of their theological implications, and especially of their psycho-religious impact.

In reading most of Hopkins' poetry, I have found it heavily informed by Christian theology structured by Ignatian spiritual methods. This influence, strikingly manifest in his first major poem, "The Wreck of the Deutschland," is clearly evident in much of the mature poetry of the Jesuit period except those sonnets of the last years usually designated as the "terrible sonnets." These I have tried to show as presenting a special problem both in relation to Hopkins' life and art. The nature of the Ignatian influence is shown to be that of providing the poet with an ordered and intelligible world view, with an approach to nature, man, and God, and lastly, with emotional and mental predispositions convertible to poetic techniques. The main treatment of this shaping of Hopkins' vision is done in Chapter Two. I urge readers (except those intrepid seekers ready to grapple with abstruse origins) to bypass this section in favor of the explanations that follow.

The findings of my efforts tend to second those readers who see Hopkins a priest-poet at his best; however, despite the pervasive influences of Ignatian spirituality which I found, I do not wish to suggest that the priest and poet were always in equilibrium, or that the domination of the priest was always good for the poet. Though I have accepted the historical epithet in Hopkins criticism, *priest-poet,* I do feel that it is a misnomer, for little of Hopkins' poetry is priestly in any denotative sense while most of it is religious in very special senses. Most of these special implications, I have tried to show, are either directly inspired or profoundly informed by Ignatian methods of spirituality. Even though the Ignatian view is a major pattern in this study, every effort has been made to keep the poet and his art in the foreground; a fuller reading of Hopkins is the main objective.

There are some objections that might be forestalled at the outset. One is that I have been uncritical in my thesis and have overstated it. I have tried in this study to immerse myself in the Spiritual Exercises and then read Hopkins' poetry. I am quite aware that I have read it with a singular eye. I have done so because I believe that the Spiritual Exercises are that central to Hopkins' art. It should not be thought that by treating my theme so positively I do accept uncritically either Ignatius as a spiritual guide or Hopkins as a poet. My demurs here are considerably less important than my thesis. Moreover Hopkins lived Ignatian spirituality faithfully all his life, a fact the implications of which no reader can ignore whatever his attitude towards Catholicism and the Society of Jesus.

It might also be objected that since Ignatius and Hopkins were both Christians, quite naturally they shared a common view. I am quite aware of this though it should be added that historians of religion discern such traditions as Ignatian or Augustinian or Thomistic Christianity. What I have tried to do is parallel Hopkins' views and manners as a poet with the Spiritual Exercises so as to show their consonance, thereby indicating the degree to which Hopkins shared Ignatius' view of Christianity, and suggesting that this harmony informed Hopkins' art to an imposing extent. A richer reading of his poetry, it is hoped, will be afforded through an awareness of this key factor.

My debts are many, and in general I wish to thank everyone who helped me in any way. I am especially grateful to Dr. James Hall who saw the book through its first version; to the many members of the Society of Jesus of the Oregon Province who answered my countless questions, lent me books and materials by the score, including matter in their archives, and kindly provided me with criticisms even when I rejected some of their evaluations and perspectives. I wish to especially thank the Reverend D. A. Bischoff, S.J., who through a period of some eight years has generously shared his voluminous collection of Hopkins with me, has put in my hands any scholarship relevant to my endeavors, and, most of all, has imparted to me large parts of what I consider to be the most comprehensive knowledge of Hopkins' life possessed by any scholar. I am indebted to him for the new biographical facts of which I have made use. Of course, the way I have made use of them as well as any other scholarship is entirely my own responsibility and any error must redound to me.

I am grateful to the following publishers who so kindly permitted me to quote books that they have published: Oxford University Press, The Newman Press, Sheed and Ward Inc., Chatto and Windus, Ltd., Yale University Press, The Bruce Publishing Company, The Catholic Book Publishing Company. Finally I wish to express my appreciation to the Very Reverend A. A. Lemieux, S.J., President of Seattle University, for his kind interest in my work and through whose efforts the Western Gear Foundation generously granted me a subvention for publication.

Seattle,
January, 1959   D. A. DOWNES

CHAPTER ONE

Elected Silence:
Gerard Manley Hopkins, 1844-1889

Gerard Manley Hopkins was born at Stratford, Essex, July 28, 1844. He was the eldest of Manley and Kate Smith Hopkins' nine children. Manley was a man of some refinement and sensitivity who tried to write poetry. Kate Hopkins was a rather quiet person whose nice restraint belied a quick and analytic mind. The two parents shared with their family a lively interest in poetry, music, and painting. They also held in common a belief in a pliable Anglicanism, at a time when the plasticity of traditional Christianity was being given its severest tests.

About 1852, the family moved to a quiet London suburb, Hampstead. Gerard attended Highgate School until 1863. Gerard's childhood was ordinary in that he was fostered on those mores usual to a middle class household in the nineteenth century. The world seemed to offer great individual promise and thus there was an aura of adventure about finding a place in it. Gerard possessed the ordinary amount of adolescent derring-do. There is a story told about him while at Highgate which is some indication of his moral courage. After a discussion about the physical hardships of seamen, Gerard announced that he was prepared to undergo an endurance test by going for an extended length of time without any form of liquid. The exact length of time is not clear, but it was of considerable duration, for he held out until he collapsed. However, he lost the bet through the interference of the headmaster.

While at Highgate, Gerard won an Exhibition (scholarship) to Balliol College, Oxford. Attendance at Oxford plunged him into the wake of the Oxford Movement whose waning spirit still moved Oxford dons. This atmosphere must have sharpened a religious crisis in young Hopkins which had its basis in his moral anxiety during puberty augmented by his confessor's faulty advice of keeping written records of his failings, a potentially disastrous practice for one of scrupulous conscience.

Despite this turmoil, Gerard showed strong attraction to painting and was writing rather competent verse notable for its awareness of Shakespeare, Milton, and Keats. He was showing brilliance as a classical scholar. However, his moral and spiritual problems remained his prime concern, and before he left Oxford, reached the stage of crisis which ended in 1866 when John Henry Newman received him into the Roman Catholic Church.

The details of his conversion are revealing. On August 28, 1866, Hopkins wrote to Newman to arrange an interview to ask advice about being received into the Roman Church. He was still at his studies at Balliol, looking forward to his last terms. He wrote in part:

> Rev. Sir,
> I address you with great hesitation, knowing that you are in the midst of your own engagements and because you must be exposed to applications from all sides. I am anxious to become a Catholic, and I thought that you might possibly be able to see me for a short time when I pass through Birmingham in a few days, I believe on Friday. But I feel most strongly the injustice of intruding on your engagements or convenience and therefore, if that is the case, I shall think it a favour if you will kindly let me know that you are unable to see me. I do not want to be helped to any conclusions of belief, for I am thankful to say that my mind is made up, but the necessity of becoming a Catholic (although I have long foreseen where the only consistent position would lie) coming on me suddenly has put me into painful confusion of mind about my immediate duty in my circumstances. . . . I say this much to take from you any hesitation in not al-

lowing me to come to Birmingham if duties should
stand in the way: you will understand that by God's
mercy I am clear as to the sole authority of the Church
of Rome.[1]

Some weeks later, Newman replied:

My dear Sir,
I am sorry I was abroad when your letter came. Now
I am returned and expect to be here for some weeks.
I will gladly see you as you propose, if you will fix
a day.[2]

Though Hopkins was received into the Church on October
21, 1866, there is little genuine evidence as to the actual time
of this conversion. All that has been published is a letter to
a close friend, the Rev. E. W. Urquhart, an Anglican priest,
five years his senior. This letter is significant not only because
it refers to Hopkins' conversion explicitly, but also because it
makes clear that there was no duress in his decision:

In fact as I told you my conversion when it came was
all in a minute. Again I could not say that your talk
influenced me in that direction: to see or hear "Ro-
manising" things would throw me back on the English
Church as a rule. In fact it is almost implied by what
I have told you that for a good time past I have been
uninfluenced by anybody, especially from the Catholic
side.[3]

In another letter to the same friend, Hopkins remarks that
though his conversion is two months past, he had a "silent
conviction" about his conversion for almost a year.[4]
After his initial letter to Newman, it is clear that the two
met twice. Their correspondence shows how firm Hopkins'
decision was and how gentle and understanding was Newman's
treatment. Hopkins wrote a long letter to Robert Bridges telling
him about his first meeting with Newman:

Dr. Newman was most kind, I mean in the very best
sense, for his manner is not that of solicitous kindness,

but genial and almost, so to speak, unserious. And
if I may say so, he was so sensible. He asked questions
which made it clear for me how to act; I will tell you
presently what that is: he made sure I was acting de-
liberately and wished to hear my arguments; when I
had given them and said I cd. see no way out of them,
he laughed and said "Nor can I". . . . in no way did
he urge me on, rather the other way. . . . I am to go
over from Oxford to the Oratory for my reception next
term—early in the term I must make it, and since a
Retreat is advisable for a convert, Dr. Newman was
so very good as to offer me to come there at Xtmas.[5]

There was much need for firmness of purpose and for kindness in the matter. This religious transition was to prove quite
painful. Hopkins wrote home to inform his parents. Their
reaction was quick. In a letter to Newman dated October 15,
Hopkins made it very clear:

Very Reverend Father,
I have been up at Oxford just long enough to have
heard from my father and mother in return for my
letter announcing my conversion. Their answers are
terrible: I cannot read them twice. If you will pray
for them and me just now I shall be deeply thankful.
But what I am writing for is this—they urge me with
the utmost entreaties to wait till I have taken my degree—more than half a year. Of course it is impossible,
and since it is impossible to wait as long as they wish
it seems to me useless to wait at all. Would you therefore wish me to come to Birmingham at once, on Thurs-
day, Friday, or Saturday? You will understand why I
have any hesitation at all, namely therefore if im-
mediately after their letters urging a long delay I
am received without any, it would be another blow
and look like intentional cruelty.[6]

Manley Hopkins, Gerard's father, hastily wrote to H. P.
Liddon, a High Church leader at Oxford, who had been
Hopkins' advisor and with whom Gerard was on intimate terms

as their letters indicate. Liddon was asked to help prevent
Hopkins from going over to Rome. Liddon responded by writing a series of four letters urging delay and reconsideration, all
to no avail.

It was during this time that Hopkins received a bitter and
indignant letter from Dr. E. B. Pusey, who was again decrying
the loss of one more to Rome. Pusey had great admiration for
Hopkins both as a person and as a student. Some biographers
state that it was Pusey who styled Hopkins "The Star of Balliol,"
but no authoritative evidence has ever been given for such a
description.

On the same day Pusey's letter arrived, Newman wrote to
Hopkins, "It is not wonderful that you should not be able to
take so great a step without trouble and pain."[7] Hopkins went
to Birmingham, and as the entry in Newman's diary records:
"Oct. 21. Mr. Hopkins came from Oxford and was received."

Hopkins spent the time following his conversion preparing
for Greats at Oxford, attempting to adjust to his newly adopted
faith, and trying to soothe family feelings. There was still an
important decision to be made, one which he had in mind
very soon after he became a Catholic: whether he had a vocation to the priesthood, and if so, to what order of the Church.
He reflected for almost two years on this matter before he
entered the Jesuit novitiate.

Newman, cautioning him not to rush into anything, offered
him a position at the Oratory School following the completion
of his studies at Oxford. In the Trinity term, Hopkins took a
double first in Greats, and on September 13, 1867, he went
to the Oratory School as a Master.

The following Christmas Hopkins did not return to the
Oratory. In a letter (January 9, 1868) to his friend, Robert
Bridges, he explained why he was not returning. Bridges was
just about to leave on a trip to Cairo:

> This note accordingly is to say goodbye. The year
> you will be away I have no doubt will make a great
> difference in my position though I cannot know exactly
> what. But the uncertainty I am in about the future is

so very unpleasant and so breaks my power of apply-
ing to anything that I am resolved to end it, which
I shall do by going into a retreat at Easter at the latest
and deciding whether I have a vocation to the priesthood. Do not repeat this.[8]

Hopkins made the retreat on April 27, 1868, at the Jesuit
Novitiate, Roehampton, under the direction of Father Henry
Coleridge, S.J. During this retreat he decided to study for
the priesthood, bringing to a close a year and a half of delibera-
tion. Apparently he gave some consideration to entering the
Benedictines, but how much we do not know. He decided to
enter the Society of Jesus, was examined on May 9 by the
Jesuit provincial, Father Alfred Weld, and received his acceptance on May 30. Newman received the decision with approval and congratulation:

> I am both surprised and glad at your news. . . . I
> think it is the very thing for you. You are quite out,
> in thinking that when I offered you a "home" here, I
> dreamed of your having a vocation for us. This I
> clearly saw you had *not,* from the moment you came
> to us. Don't call "the Jesuit Discipline" hard, it will
> bring you to heaven. The Benedictines would not have
> suited you.
>
> Ever yours affectionately,
> John H. Newman[9]

Hopkins began his study on September 7, 1868. Before his
entrance, he burned most of the poetry he had written. This
was not demanded of him, but he did so as an act of total
dedication to his chosen life, foreshadowing the strife that was
to take place between the priest and artist in him. At this
time, he resolved never to write again unless "by the wish of
my superiors."

At Manresa he began the first steps of the long arduous
Jesuit training. Hopkins was here as a novice for two years,
during which time he devoted himself entirely to a routine
of attending mass, meditating, reading spiritual books, and

conferring with his spiritual director. His only other activities were menial tasks, such as sweeping floors, washing dishes, and the like, with occasional holiday visits to churches and museums in London. It is during this time that the novice makes his first "Long Retreat," a four-week period devoted exclusively to prayer, meditation, and self-examination. The novice is introduced to the *Spiritual Exercises of St. Ignatius,* in large measure the basis of his spiritual life during the time of preparation for reception of vows as well as throughout his remaining life as a Jesuit. The phrase *Long Retreat* simply describes the Exercises in their entirety.

It is general knowledge among retreat masters that these initial thirty days of reflection, devotion, and election are a genuine test of the Jesuit vocation. It is at this time that the Jesuit character is formed, a task which is the main work of the two years in the novitiate, culminating in the taking of first vows. Hopkins took his in 1870 and went off to begin the second stage, his philosophical studies at St. Mary's Hall, Stonyhurst, where he studied three years. Finishing in 1873, he returned to Manresa House where he taught the Classics for one year. This readied him for the next step, his theological studies at St. Beuno's College in North Wales.

While at St. Beuno's, late in the year 1875, his superior, Father James Jones, suggested that he write about the terrible tragedy of the *Deutschland* wreck in which five German nuns were drowned. After nearly seven years' silence, Hopkins wrote a long ode which he called, "The Wreck of the Deutschland," an imposing example of the poetic creativity that had welled up in him. After this, he felt freer to write poetry though he had a tender conscience all his life about giving his time and energy to it. His periods of composition were spasmodic, but despite the shortness of his life, he left a substantial number of sonnets and lyrics, which, if not distinguished by their number, are rare in their descriptive beauty and depth of religious implication. The strangest note, perhaps, about them is the means by which his verse was finally published, thereby bringing to their author a posthumous literary fame despite the final consignment of his efforts to an almost certain oblivion.

Hopkins was ordained a priest in 1877, but was not permitted to take the usual additional year of theological study because of his poor showing in the theological examinations. While undoubtedly part of this difficulty was due to his infirm health, his superiors may have very well taken into account Hopkins' preference for the writings of the great Franciscan thinker, John Duns Scotus, over the scholasticism of Suarez, their current guide in matters theological and philosophical. This judgment may have cut down a brilliant theological career, for Hopkins' personal papers reveal a mind that had brilliant theological flashes and insights. Whatever the case, this was the first important setback in his career.

His assignments involved parish work and teaching in London, Liverpool, Glasgow, Oxford, and Stonyhurst College. Hopkins was never robust, being constantly subject to various minor ailments so that he was barely equal to the normal duties of a Jesuit. A story he told on himself indicates his difficulties as a preacher. While struggling through a sermon on a sweltering summer's day, he noticed that members of the congregation frequently used their handkerchiefs. For once, he thought, he had been effective, even moving some to tears. Apparently he labored under this illusion throughout the rest of his talk, only later to discover that the handkerchief users were mopping their brows! When one reads through the sermons that are extant, one is often struck by their fresh theological perspectives, the courage of the preacher in attacking difficult sermon topics, and a frequent brilliance and beauty of composition. On the other hand, given Hopkins' short stature and high-pitched voice in addition to a chronic inability to estimate his congregation, it comes as no surprise that his preaching came to nought. One wonders what a working class congregation made of his sermon on the Sacred Heart with all of its word-play on *heart,* or the reaction of a high-society congregation to his use of a cow's udder and teats as an *exemplum* for the Church and the seven sacraments. However, these moments ought not be made heavy tragedy. It must not be forgotten that Hopkins had an abiding sense of humor (he often supplied the comic entertainment for his colleagues) which certainly must have lightened such episodes.

Hopkins' last assignment, 1884, took him to University College in Dublin. The Jesuits had been called upon to save the remnants of Newman's Catholic University, to which end Father William Delaney hurriedly gathered a staff of French, English, and Irish Jesuits. Hopkins was assigned the Chair of Classics, for which he had more than enough learning but little ability in classroom teaching. Moreover, the assignment was one he had to undertake out of sheer obedience, as the notes, letters, and poems of the Dublin period make clear.

There are some stories told about him as a teacher. One is about a class in Homer in which he, being unable to engage his class, ordered one of his smaller students[10] to lie down on the floor. Hopkins then took him by his heels and with great effort dragged him about the room to illustrate Hector in relation to the walls of Troy! Another story that is revealing of his incapacity for the burdens of the pedagogue is the one about his being discovered in the early morning hours, swathed in towels, figuring the grades of the semi-annual examinations of his students into fractions. This state of exhaustion and nervous fatigue was not unusual to him, especially during the Dublin years, and he strangely was unable to see even the most obvious remedy to many of his ills, as, for example, his eyes from which he suffered a great deal, but never sought adequate medical care.

He was not only ineffective as a teacher. As a scholar, he had envisioned as least five works, three in prose and two in verse. But getting little positive encouragement from his superiors, a push he seems to have needed inordinately, these projects got nowhere. More seriously, he seems to have finally given up hope for any official approval of his poetic endeavors, an approval and acknowledgment that he dearly wanted but never asked for. Though he resolved to the end to make this sacrifice and admirably kept his resolution, the gradual death of his poetic inspiration is tragic, the more so since it was really uncalled for. However, the call Hopkins heard may not have been ordinary.[11]

Outwardly, Hopkins' last years were filled with interests both artistic and intellectual, but inwardly he experienced recurring periods of desolation. His continuing bad health, his inability to bring any of his pursuits to any real completion, arduousness of his teaching duties, to which must be added a frequently fruitless spiritual life, made these years unbalanced with tensions, weaknesses, and frustrations. He recorded some of these moments in the sonnets dubbed "terrible" because they were born of grief and suffering, "unbidden and against my will."

Hopkins contracted typhoid fever in the spring of 1889. He was given every medical attention, but with the onset of peritonitis, he died with his parents at his side. After having received the Last Sacraments and shortly before he died, he was heard whispering, "I am so happy, so happy." His funeral at St. Francis Xavier's, Gardner Street, was well attended, after which he was buried at Glasnevin on the outskirts of Dublin. Those who knew him held him in esteem because of his gentleness and kindness, which is to say his genuine goodness. Here it might have all ended were it not that he left a rich legacy of some of the rarest and finest writing in English, which was to find its curious way in this world.

Every year a Jesuit makes a retreat, in which again he employs the Spiritual Exercises as regenerative factor to renew within himself the basic ideas of his Order. Father Hugo Rahner, a leading student of Ignatian spirituality, wrote, "It is a long-established fact of history that the character and thought of Ignatius found their clearest expression in the book of Spiritual Exercises and that his Order arose and is ever freshly renewed from that world of thought."[12]

From 1868 the Spiritual Exercises were an integral part of Gerard Hopkins' life. They became the rule and guide of his whole being. As Dr. John Pick, a noted Hopkins scholar put it:

For twenty-one years Hopkins dedicated himself to the Society of Jesus; for twenty-one years he studied, meditated, and practiced the Spiritual Exercises. They became part of his life and attitude. They gave direction to all he experienced, thought, and wrote. They influenced his most exuberant and joyous poems; they were part of his sufferings and desolation. He delivered sermons suggested by them, started to write a commentary on them; he gave them to others. They fashioned his reaction to nature and beauty. Their echo is found in his consciousness of imperfection, in his abnegation and in the integrity with which he faced hardship and disappointment. His attitude toward poetry and fame was shaped by them. They moulded his native temperament and sensibility to an ideal of perfection. Without knowing something of them we can hardly know the priest-poet.[13]

Clearly, an approach to Gerard Manley Hopkins, the man or poet, ought to include a close study and analysis of the one document that did more than anything else to change his life. Though it was evident that he had a natural ascetic bent, nevertheless it was the Spiritual Exercises that were the basis of his asceticism and guided it along paths that provided his religious sensibility with a fully flowered perspective. The result was that the vision of Ignatius became substantially Hopkins' vision of which his poetry is a lasting testament.

Critics and biographers of Gerard Manley Hopkins have often noted that Hopkins' poetic career falls into two segments: the brilliant and talented youth at Oxford and the ascetic Jesuit priest-poet. They have often said that the greatest influences on the mature poetry of the Jesuit period certainly would be the instrument for spirituality that St. Ignatius Loyola wrote at Manresa, *The Spiritual Exercises.* But few studies have attempted a careful analysis of Hopkins' poetry, early and late, primarily from the vantage point of Ignatian spirituality. This work undertakes to describe the Ignatian spirit and study the Hopkins canon for evidences of its influence.

CHAPTER TWO

Ignatius and Hopkins

". . .—for Christ plays in ten thousand places. . ."

Before getting some idea of Hopkins' personal formulation
of Ignatian spirituality, it is necessary for us to recapitulate
the ground and growth of his thought up to the time that he
wrote his notes on the Spiritual Exercises. The digression faces
us because the very speculations he related to the spiritual ideals
of Ignatius had their roots and development in his early thinking. Briefly sketched, his theories amount to an attempt to
erect a philosophy of being, a system of sensation, a process of
knowing, a natural theology, and an anatomy of beauty. My
interest is to draw up the lines of Hopkins' thought until the
advent of Ignatian spirituality. The source and inspiration of
his notions will claim little of my attention.

Following the chronology of Hopkins' intellectual development, the first awareness to take form was his philosophy of
beauty. In his youth he had cultivated his senses to keenness and
delicateness under the influence of John Ruskin and the Pre-
Raphaelite school. The guiding notion was a lucid perception
of the object, both the real existent and the ideal type. His
whole bent was to discover the laws of beauty and their counter-
parts in artistic principles. His diaries and sketchbooks are
filled with the minute recordings of nature predominately
from the perspectives of sound and light. The bent of his endeavor seemed to be a formulation of esthetic principles along
physical, mathematical, and metaphysical lines.

His study and practice led him to theorize on the nature of
sensation itself. Having the artistic desire to elucidate the

spiritual in art and nature, Hopkins entertained the view that clear and intense sensation was possible only by means of highly active and intensely spiritualized senses. This being the case, then the observer, being a focal point, could lucidly affix a moment in nature's flux, and penetrate to the spiritual ideal within the real fact. To give order and precision to his notion of beauty, he asserted a Platonic idealism by which every set form in nature derived from an ideal reality in which the type had the highest development. Such a theory rested on a metaphysical basis of Idealism, by which Hopkins countered the materialist Realism of his day, based on the physical sciences, which posited a reality in flux with only accidental types. Despite his desire to lay down a "science" of art and beauty, Hopkins' attempt got no nearer his goal than a quasi-mathematical fixed scale of absolute forms. Absolute forms forced him out of physics and into Platonic metaphysics.

After his Oxford days, Hopkins crystallized his thinking. His esthetic practice of recording nature types both in word and line, plus his visionary philosophical speculations on beauty, led him to epitomize his views by means of two complicated coinages, "inscape" and "instress." These two terms, now as famous as puzzling, denote respectively Hopkins' notion of absolute forms scaled in the flux of nature, and the unifying force of being within the fixed type, which is the communicative force between object and subject as well as the emotive response within the subject.[1] The emphasis should be placed on unity of being. Unity implies an order, a structure, an organization. For Hopkins, beauty lies in the part relationships and the part-whole. Each entity has a unity that flows down from its ideal form, whole to part, part to part. The sensible quality of this unity is the virtue of "inscape." This is confirmed by Hopkins in this passage on beauty and inscape. Speaking of verse he wrote: "But if it has a meaning and is meant to be heard for its own sake it will be poetry if you take poetry to be a kind of composition and not the virtue or excellence of that kind, as eloquence is the virtue of oratory and not oratory only and beauty the virtue of inscape and not inscape only."[2]

In an examination of the senses in which Hopkins employed the term, it is clear that the prefix "in" of "inscape" denotes that "scape" is the outer fixed shape of the intrinsic form of a thing. For this reason Hopkins was not satisfied with the terms design and pattern as the unqualified designation of the intrinsic order of being. These terms indicate an order impressed from without, an extrinsic principle of unity. Further it is quite possible that an order of a thing be perceived which is no more than its pattern while no inscape can be discovered. There are many passages in Hopkins' papers which show the use of "inscape" and its difference from design or shape. Here are two: "Spanish chestnuts: their inscape here bold, jutty, somewhat oak-like, attractive, the branching visible and the leaved peaks spotted so as to make crests of eyes."[3] "The Horned Violet is a pretty thing, gracefully lashed. Even in withering the flower ran through beautiful inscapes by the screwing up of the petals into straight little barrels or tubes."[4] However, the most important note about "inscape" is its etymological suggestion of "shape" and "creation," so that he designates the "scapes" of the world as emblems of God's dynamic creativity. This facet becomes an important link with his Ignatian spirituality in his later thinking.

The other term, "instress," is a word that appears many times in his writing. As a philosophical term, it means the principle of actuality in a thing, the perfection of being proper to a thing. It is a principle of being which keeps a thing in existence. Hopkins has substituted this term for the Scholastic term *actus.* He often employs "instress" as a verb which carries the idea of "to actualize," to bring into being: "And as mere possibility, passive power, is not power proper and has no activity it cannot of itself come to stress, cannot instress itself."[5] Again the prefix "in" emphasizes its intrinsicality. Also it is notable that the term "stress" expresses more effectively that energy by which, as Hopkins put it, "all things are upheld,"[6] and strains after their continued existence. When the prefix "dis" is added to "stress," Hopkins meant the loss of the perfection of being proper to a thing. This is what happened to the rebellious angels: "It would seem that their fall was at once the attack of Michael and their own act: Michael and his angels instressed and distressed them with the thought of their unlikeness to the Most High."[7] He also added the prefix "out" to "stress": "The first intention then of God outside himself or, as they say, *ad extra,* outwards, the first outstress of God's power was Christ."[8] Here outstress is the coming to stress out from self. This insight becomes fundamental in his last thoughts.

Now what relationship does instress have with inscape? Father Peters attempted a clarification.

Placing "instress" by the side of "inscape" we note that the instress will strike the poet as the force that holds the inscape together; it is for him the power that ever actualizes the inscape. Further, we observe that in the act of perception the inscape is known first and in this grasp of the inscape is felt the stress of being behind it, is felt its instress. I speak of "feeling the instress" and I do so with good reason. Inscape, being a sensitive manifestation of a being's individuality, is perceived by the senses; but instress, though given in the perception of inscape, is not directly perceived by the senses, because it is not a primary sensible quality of the thing. Hence it follows that, while inscape can be described, however imperfectly, in terms of sense-impressions, instress cannot, but must be interpreted in terms of its impression on the soul, in terms, that is, of *affects* of the soul. We can now understand why and how it is that "instress" in Hopkins's writings stands for two distinct and separate things, related to each other as cause and effect; as a cause "instress" refers for Hopkins to that core of being or inherent energy which is the actuality of the object; as effect "instress" stands for the specifically individual impression the object makes on man.[9]

While this seems to be the general notion, in the light of Hopkins' insistence on absolute forms, the phrase in the 9th line of quotation, "manifestation of a being's individuality," ought to be modified to read, "of a being's unique form or type."

Also emphasis should be placed in the 13th and 14th lines on "imperfectly," since seeing the inscape of a thing is a special kind of perception. Finally, the last portion of the quotation is important because instress is the communicative and evocative element of being.

Basically, Hopkins' poetic theory related to inscape. He stated it simply in a letter to Bridges, February 15, 1879, which, because of its late date suggests that, fundamentally, Hopkins never altered this notion: "But as air, melody, is what strikes me most of all in music and design in painting, so design, pattern or what I am in the habit of calling 'inscape' is what I above all aim at in poetry."[10] Poetry, then, expresses essences in concrete form. Poetic inscape bears the image of the special types of things as well as the creative form of the poet, that is mankind. A poem such as Hopkins' "Henry Purcell" represents Hopkins' poetic inscape of Purcell's musical inscapes. Thus as reader, we are presented with Hopkins' discovery of the genius of Purcell in Purcell's music which, according to Hopkins' inscape, sounds the universal creativity of all mankind as well as Purcell himself. Hopkins' poetic expression of the inscape of Purcell affords us an inscape of Hopkins' poetic art.

Another term of major importance for Hopkins was "pitch." While often confused with inscape, the term was really an early acquisition as a result of Hopkins' interest in light and sound as the major media of human perception, as well as a related proportionate scale of beauty. Hopkins had to account for the individual entity in nature in his philosophy of beauty. He did so by the term, "pitch," by which he meant, quite denotatively, that degree of evaluation in a scale, that refinement of organization and height of development which the various modifications of a fixed form or inscape has. This has obvious implications for the growth of awareness and perception especially for the artist. Hopkins noted that he sought in his poetry "an individualizing touch." This, it would seem, meant perceiving the inscapes of nature at their highest pitches through deeper instressing, and then uttering the vision in inscapes of heightened sound, that is, poetry.

This approach to the individuality was held by Hopkins long before he ever read anything of Duns Scotus. But it was only natural that he would search through philosophy for some justification of his attitude. He always liked the study of philosophy. As a young student at Oxford he wrote some philosophical essays which are notable for their insight and thoroughness. During these days Aristotle was his philosopher, as he wrote to Alexander Baillie in February, 1868: "This reminds me to say that I find myself in an ever prostrate admiration of Aristotle and am of the way of thinking, so far as I know him or know about him, that he is the end-all and be-all of philosophy."[11] As a Jesuit he studied philosophy for three years and the philosophy was that of Francisco Suarez, the famous Jesuit theologian. But Hopkins did not become a Suarezian, for at the end of his second year he gave himself over to Duns Scotus.[12] He wrote in his diary August 3, 1872: "At this time I had first begun to get hold of the copy of Scotus on the Sentences in the Baddely library and was flush with a new stroke of enthusiasm. It may come to nothing or it may be a mercy from God. But just then when I took in any inscape of the sky or sea I thought of Scotus."[13]

"I thought of Scotus." Why? The answer is that in the philosophy of Scotus he discovered a rather fully developed metaphysics which was highly compatible with his own views. Moreover, Scotus' speculations included theological perspectives in which Hopkins saw the possibility of yoking to the spiritual ideal of Ignatius.

What follows is no more than a sketch of Scotus. What I am interested in is indicating the similarity of some of Scotus to Hopkins' thought development in order that it will be somewhat clear why Hopkins seized on Scotism as a more mature system of his own views, and how in reading deeper into Scotus, he was led to fit into the Spiritual Exercises the theology of Scotus.

The source of Hopkins' quest was undoubtedly his intense conviction that natural beauty was mortal. Scaled nature sounding and flashing between heaven and earth ultimately descended into oblivion unless a force beyond nature revitalized and renewed it. Hopkins noted this descent and dying in his theory of sensation. While there were those moments of the stress of being which, instressed, brought elation and joy in the life of things, there were those other moments when the senses were unreceptive to the stress of being which caused suspension, relaxation, or his word, "slack." Death in senses led him to see the need for spiritualization of the senses, which is to say, to search for the extension of consciousness beyond the natural, to find immortal beauty. It can be supposed that this lay behind Hopkins' religious development, eventually leading him to the priesthood within the Catholic Church. The point is that his religious vocation was a development of his early bent, a carrying on of his original quest, for chastity of mind was a touchstone of his nature.

Hopkins read Scotus chiefly from 1872 to 1884. One can imagine how positive his reaction was as he delved. To Scotus, nature was a real being which originated in the mind of God as an idea, a prior existence to God's willing individual existence. Individual entities were so many levels of common nature. The personification of nature was Christ who was the summation of all the degrees. Now Scotus posited the notion that spiritual reality can be taken in directly through the senses by means of a kind of connection between what he called innate memory and the sense process. By means of a kind of unconscious knowing, Scotus allowed for an intimation of common nature, a kind of visionary sense experience by means of which insights could be had into the very fixed ideas in the order of nature before their individualization or selfing. Here seemed an equivalent for inscape. Moreover, such an intuitive vision afforded a glimpse into the created nature of Christ wherein all the types in common nature sought completion. This seeking or straining after the prototypic idea was a kind of creative stress from God which, when instressed by man, afforded human awareness of God behind the idea behind the real existent. Here was something very much like Hopkins' instress. Finally, Scotus provided for a very heavy Christological emphasis, for Christ could be put down as Divine Inscape, the Archetype of all created nature, whose stress was everywhere, and properly instressed, afforded a vision of Immortal Beauty. But it was left for St. Ignatius to provide the proper methods of instress.

II

When one considers the very personal stamp of Ignatius, both on the Spiritual Exercises and the Society of Jesus, it is notable that there are striking reflections of this mark on Hopkins' *Commentary*. One of the distinguishing characteristics of the Exercises is Ignatius' background: the son of an old and distinguished Spanish family who for generations lived, fought, and died for the earthly ideals of Castilian kings. Implicit in the very structure of the Society of Jesus and explicit in the Exercises are those ideals of discipline, dedication, and gallantry, which were inculcated into every member of the Loyola family since 1200. Even the spiritual ideal of the saint is still within the historical traditions of the family: the ideal of knighthood.

It is also the historical context that provides us with the truest view of the Exercises. As a man of the world, Ignatius was born into the manner of chivalry. He conceived his main life endeavors to be exalted service of an earthly king. When one examines the transformation that came over that wounded knight, a most striking fact appears. Ignatius did not change his ideals. He was first and always a chivalrous knight. What happened was that his ideals were raised from the service of an earthly king to a divine king, and the quality of service was elevated from that of the natural plane to the supernatural. The Ignatian ideal is expressed most significantly in the Exercises in the meditations on the Kingdom of Christ and the Two Standards. You might say that in these Exercises Ignatius, the captain, drew up an oath for a company of men to pledge themselves to serve under the standard of Christ, the King, with unstinted devotion and unlimited sacrifice. The enemy is the desert fox himself, Satan. The terms are unconditional surrender.

In true military fashion, the Ignatian battle plans call for the strategy of the "retreat." By having the company of Jesus withdraw from battle for a spell, it acquires its most potent of weapons, "a generous heart inflamed by the love of God." Every year of his life, the Jesuit puts aside his usual tasks in order to re-examine his life in the light of Ignatian spirituality, and then rededicate himself to greater service in the Kingdom of Christ against the Kingdom of Satan.

Hopkins, of course, made yearly retreats and, like many another Jesuit, he often made notes which recorded his personal impressions of and reflections on the Spiritual Exercises. During these retreats, at least between 1878 and 1885, he used a copy of the Exercises translated from the original Spanish by the Father General John Roothaan. The title was *Exercitia Spiritualia S. P. Ignatii de Loyola cum Versione Litterali ex Autographo Hispanico Notis Illustrata Addita Appendice De Ratione Meditandi Editio Parisiensis Prima juxta Romanam Editionem Quintam I. H. S. Lutetiae Parisiorum.* He used an interleaved copy in which he made notes on various sections of the exercises over several years. According to the late editor of Hopkins' papers, Humphry House, the greatest part of these was made during the Long Retreat of his Tertianship (November-December, 1881).[14]

In a sidenote in the interleaved copy, Hopkins refers to a "rough draft of the *Commentary* for the Provincial" which would indicate that he had intended to write a full-length commentary on the Exercises and for this reason he steadily made notes on various sections of the Exercises. The rough draft is not extant, but among his papers, he left us in his Roothaan about ninety-two pages of detailed comment which more than likely would have been incorporated into his commentary. In a letter to Robert Bridges on September 26, 1882, Hopkins mentioned this project: "I did in my last week at Roehampton write 16 pages of a rough draft of a commentary on St. Ignatius' Spiritual Exercises. This work would interest none but a Jesuit, but to me it is interesting enough and, as you see, it is very professional."[15]

To see life and see it whole became for Hopkins to see Christ. The *Commentary* is really a development of this notion: Christ as the prototypic pattern of creation (Foundation);

Christ and Fallen Nature in the First Week; the Incarnate
Christ and the stress of grace in the Second Week; Christ's
great sacrifice in the Third and Fourth Weeks. This focus could
not be more Ignatian. The Ignatian ideal was the knighthood
of Christ, the King, whose service is accomplished through the
elevation of supernatural grace. This is fully consonant with
the historical genesis of Ignatian spirituality, for it is recorded
that it was in the mystical graces that Ignatius experienced by
the river Cardoner, that he was given a greater standard under
which to serve, a call to recruit a new arm, and a super oath
of allegiance to the most awesome of kings to win, truly, the
war to end all wars. Finally, Hopkins looked to Scotus and
wherever possible tried to co-relate them with the discipline
of Ignatius.

Hopkins' attempt to describe a complete cosmology of both
naturality and supernaturality, which is the goal to which his
thinking led him, was never fully completed. However his
spiritual writings contain the main outlines of the final dispositions of his thought. And the *Commentary* in particular
contains the central design. The first consideration, of course,
was creation. Ignatius began his Exercises by setting down a
kind of foundation on which rested the whole structure of his
spiritual discipline. The first words, "Man was created to praise,"
is the key of Ignatian spirituality. Hopkins started here to put
down his scheme of salvation.

The *Commentary* opens with a long philosophical examination of the first three words of the Principle or Foundation
of the Exercises: *Homo creatus est.* The discussion examines
three alternative propositions: chance as the source of man's
existence, man as the source of his own being, and some extrinsic power the cause of man's being. Hopkins disposes of
the first two possibilities largely in the Scholastic manner and
posits the third point, that man is due to an extrinsic power.

Now the important consideration about himself was his distinctiveness, his *self*. It is to selfness that he finally turned his
greatest attention. He had already directed his attention to
aspects of being, inscape and instress, but now he faced real
existents, unified being, self-being. Another way of noting his

interest is to say that he turned his attention to pitch—his own term—which, it will be recalled, designated that degree of individuation in the order of nature. Again he turned to Scotus.

Scotus had a notion and a word for this very problem. For he distinguished in a real entity a generic form, a specific form, and an individual form (which correspond to the logical determinations in the mind, the generic, specific, and individual). These were not separate entities, but distinct features of one being. Through the addition of a specific difference the specific form derives from the generic, and by the addition of a difference that individualizes, the individual form arises from the specific. This final determination of the object to its specific essence Scotus called its "thisness," *haecceitas,* a rough equivalent for pitch. Father Peters points out, "Thus while in the philosophy of Aristotle and St. Thomas there is no separate entity which limits the universal, determines and individualizes it, there is such a separate entity in the theory of Scotus. . . ."[16] Further, it is to be noted that in virtue of this individualizing principle, all created things are active, for this principle being "form" is active. Again his theory was compatible with Hopkins' notion of being as always acting, stressing. Man's origin and existence was due to some extrinsic power. The proof was that finite existence postulates the existence of infinite being. Using Scotus' proof, Hopkins still left intact his notions of inscape, instress, and pitch (though pitch does not seem to be an accurate equivalent for Scotus' notion).

Here is Hopkins' eloquent version of Scotus. Because the passage indicates how significant the notion "self" became for him, I am quoting a large portion of the opening section of the *Commentary*:

> We may learn that all things are created by consideration of the world without or of ourselves the world within. The former is the consideration usually dwelt on, but the latter takes on the mind more hold. I find myself both as man and as myself something most determined and distinctive, at pitch, more distinctive and higher pitched than anything else I see; I find

myself with my pleasures and pains, my powers and my
experiences, my deserts and guilt, my shame and sense
of beauty, my dangers, hopes, fears, and all my fate,
more important to myself than anything I see. And
when I ask where does all this throng and stack of
being, so rich, so distinctive, so important, come from,
nothing I see can answer me. And this whether I speak
of human nature or of my individuality, my selfbeing.
For human nature, being more highly pitched, selved,
and distinctive than anything in the world, can have
been developed, evolved, condensed, from the vastness of the world not anyhow or by the working of
common powers but only by one of finer or higher
pitch and determination than itself and certainly than
any that elsewhere we see, for this power had to force
forward the starting or stubborn elements to the one
pitch required.

He goes on to point out that if his manhood seems most distinctive, that part of his nature which most distinguishes him,
his reason, is unique. Man is the best proof for the existence
of God:

And this is much more true when we consider the
mind; when I consider my selfbeing, my consciousness
and feeling of myself, that taste of myself, of I and *me*
above and in all things, which is more distinctive than
the taste of ale or alum, more distinctive than the smell
of walnutleaf or camphor, and is incommunicable by
any means to another man (as when I was a child I
used to ask myself: What must it be to be someone
else?). Nothing else in nature comes near this unspeak-
able stress of pitch, distinctiveness, and selving, this
selfbeing of my own. Nothing explains it or resembles
it, except so far as this, that other men to themselves
have the same feeling. But this only multiplies the
phenomena to be explained so far as the cases are like
and do resemble. But to me there is no resemblance:
searching nature I taste *self* but at one tankard, that of
my own being. The development, refinement, con-
densation of nothing shows any sign of being able to

match this to me or give me another taste of it, a taste
even resembling it.[17]

Of all creatures, man is the only one made in the image of
the Creator. Only man's self was raised to the dignity of a free
nature. As noted in the long passage just quoted, Hopkins
argues that the marked dignity and unique individuality of
man's nature could only be produced by "one of finer or
higher pitch and determination than itself." Here again the
influence of Scotus can be seen. Scotus put forward the theory
that God and creatures can be included in the same metaphysical genus, they both have a concept of being that is univocal. "The distinction between them is that of being *per se*
and being *per participationem.* The being of God and of
creatures are, therefore, not the same, but Scotus wishes to
express the idea that the same term, being, when applied to
God, has the same meaning as in its application to creatures,
though in the former case, it means much more. In the creature,
being is limited by the fact that a creature is finite; it is this,
not that. God, on the other hand, is unlimited and infinite.
Finitude is the intrinsic mode of being applicable to the
creature, whilst infinity belongs to God alone."[18] Most Scholastic philosophers would argue that this tends towards panthe-
ism.[19] Still it obviously bolsters the argument that the distinctiveness of man's nature would require a more distinctive nature
to produce it, and it also reinforces a sacramental view of the
world, for according to this view the world and God possess
an univocal concept of being.

The other key notion in the Foundation of the Spiritual
Exercises is that which is called the proper use of creatures.
Ignatius' point is that creatures should lead back to Creator.
Now according to Scotus' conception of creation this is theo-
logically true. For God at first possessed the idea of nature in
his mind, a perfect species in imitation of the divine essence.
The Second Person of the Trinity, as the begotten Son of God,
possesses all ideas and species. God provided nature with a
determination which according to His will, selved nature.
Nature, then, was an idea in the mind of God willed by Him

into self determinations, finally into actual existence as true selves. Moreover, all degrees of individuality were summed up in Christ. This invigorated a long-held notion, that the spiritual had primacy in the order of nature, as well as provided a basis for a central notion in Ignatian spirituality; creatures properly used lead to Creator. This lays before us a key perspective in Hopkins, the sacramental view of the world. It pervades the spiritual writings of his priesthood and is a major theme in the poetry he wrote as a Jesuit. It should also be recalled, according to Scotus, the first act of knowing is a kind of insight into common nature, an intuition into the Author and Exemplar of all created nature. This kind of visionary sight connects with Hopkins' notions of instressing nature through inscape. Poetic theory, psychology, philosophy of beauty, and natural theology all come together here in a grand alliance, largely through the mediation of Scotus.

To Hopkins, then, the inscapes of the world were "news of God." He wrote in this initial section of the *Commentary*: "Neither do I deny that God is so deeply present to everything . . . that it would be impossible for him but for his infinity not to be identified with them or, from the other side, impossible but for his infinity so to be present to them. This is oddly expressed, I see; I mean, a being so intimately present as God is to other things would be identified with them were it not for God's infinity or were it not for God's infinity he could not be so intimately present to things."[20] He wrote in a brief commentary on the Contemplation for Obtaining Love,[21] "All things therefore are charged with love, are charged with God and if we know how to touch them give off sparks and take fire, yield drops and flow, ring and tell of him."[22] His papers are filled with this spiritual vision of the world. For example: "I do not think I have ever seen anything more beautiful than the bluebell I have been looking at. I know the beauty of our Lord by it."[23] And: "As we drove home the stars came out thick: I leant back to look at them and my heart opening more than usual praised our Lord to and in whom all that beauty comes home."[24] The inscapes of the world lead back to their Creator. They are sacramentals.

Using creatures properly. Here is where man (whom human nature had supplied with reason making the self of man a person) had come to grief. For man had free will within pitch and nature which acted from a field of possible courses. But the condign condition of the aboriginal human will was created in grace, the divine stress within man to freely cooperate with the will of God. In the First Week of the Exercises, Ignatius confronts man with the wilful disobedience of God in the sin of the angels, of Adam and Eve, and of every sinner. In commenting on this section, Hopkins again resorted to Scotus, but elaborated on the role of Christ in these events to such an extent, that the following must be considered a cardinal point in his spiritual writings. Cryptically put, it was that creation depended on the Incarnation.

Hopkins' thoughts, as we have seen, were tending in the direction of understanding the creative stresses within the world. This culminated in the notion that God moves the world of beings according to their natures. But Ignatian spirituality confronted him with another stress, the stress of redemptive grace by which God moves man in a unique way. This is his last major consideration. The eventual disposition of this speculation lies in his concept of the heroic sacrifices of Christ.

Using Scotus' theory that the disposition of the Word was predestined apart from sin, Hopkins came to the conclusion that there would have had to be some sort of sacrifice on the part of Christ to provide him the chance of loving adoration by free choice. This led him to posit some theological notions which were unusual to say the least. There was sin, of course, three of them, as Ignatius presents them in the meditation. Hopkins then had four instances in which to explain the Incarnation.

The keynote was the sacrifice of Christ. Using Scotus' notion that Christ's humanity was the first act of the Divine will, Hopkins speculated about Christ's existence within the Blessed Trinity. This was the first mysterious circumstance within the Trinity in which Christ adores the Father. It was this procession within the Trinity which led to Christ's existence in angelic and human time, thus setting up new circumstances of adoration. The Trinity then was the mysterious source of Christ's sacrifices.

Using a speculation of Suarez, Hopkins explained the first sin, of the angels, as a revolt by Lucifer at being made aware of Christ's created nature being granted union with the godhead, a union he desired as the highest of the angels, most like God in nature. He would not admit Christ as the only perfect image of the Father, but rather looked pridefully to himself in his envy. The important note here, theologically as controversial as it is, is Hopkins' view that Christ, being already in some created form, hid himself, did not take His place at the head of angelic creation. He suggested that this existence might have been in the manner of the sacrament of the Eucharist. In any event, this was for him the first of Christ's sacrificial redemptive acts (in angelic time).

The second redemptive act of sacrifice was Christ's taking on human nature, annihilating himself as it were and becoming the servant of the godhead. This sacrifice he performed in reparation for the sin of the angels. This descent into human time brought new circumstances of love and adoration of the Father.

The third redemptive act of sacrifice was Christ's passion and death on the cross. This was in reparation for the sin of Adam and Eve and all their progeny. Moreover, having taken the position that God the Son's assumption of a created nature was a destiny apart from sin, Hopkins asserted the notion that the world of angels and men were brought into being as a means for Christ's joyful adoration of the Father.[25] Hopkins often expressed this notion in his poetry as that of the harvest of Christ. The *Deutschland* ode is an excellent example among many.

Thus it is clear that the central theme of his *Commentary* is the Blessed Trinity, the process of the Incarnation, and the redemption of the world. This theological emphasis, according to commentators both early and late, is the major theological structure of the Spiritual Exercises, and the meditative matter to which Ignatius directs the efficacy of his spiritual discipline.

Hopkins expressed these notions of Christ's sacrifice in his sermons, letters, and poetry. I find this Christological focus especially Ignatian since it dwells on a kind of divine heroism. It was Christ who magnificently gave up his divine privileges to become a creature in order to adore his Father (thereby giving us Mary); it was Christ who did not pre-empt his prerogative as supreme angel, but in the face of Lucifer's confrontation of his supremity, magnanimously accepted human nature in a world less than the angels'; it was Christ who chivalrously refused to ascend the throne as king of mankind, but rather chose to live and die as the least of men. This was the kind of supreme heroism that fired Ignatius and it is the same chivalric sacrifice that is the cardinal Christian ideal for Hopkins. The phrase, "great sacrifice," appears again and again in Hopkins' spiritual writings, a phrase with which he designated Christ's triple triumph. This is Ignatius' Christ also, the one whose kingdom he elected to serve.

III

It is the object of the Ignatian man to attain perfect love of God. This is to be achieved by conforming his will to the Divine will. He is so determined towards the Divine that he wishes to divest his own will of everything save the stress of the Divine. Ignatius put heavy emphasis on obedience when constituting his Society of Jesus. The touchstone of Ignatian obedience is this: obedience to a superior is obedience to Christ.

Perhaps it is well to recall here Ignatius' celebrated Letter on Obedience. He wrote three of them though it is the one written on March 26, 1553, which is the famous and important one. Written because of a disturbance among the Jesuits in Portugal, it contains in its closely composed 4000 words a dissertation on obedience that is, canonically and theologically, a classic of its kind. In it Ignatius reviews the value and dignity of obedience as it is found in the Old and New Testaments. He points out that obedience is the source and protection of all other virtues. It is the distinctive mark, he notes, of the Society of Jesus. This is evident in the very structure of the *Constitu-*

tions whose ten parts form the legislative order of the Society of Jesus, providing a practical and prudent regulatory system for furthering the ends of the Society as Ignatius envisioned them: a troop of evangelical soldiers, always ready and fully mobile, sworn to the service of Christ and of the Pope even to death.

Ignatius was led very soon to see the wisdom of thinking with the Church (he even drew up a set of rules for thinking with the Church), and his letter underscores his attitude. He points out that the motives for obedience can be discovered from reason and revelation. Reason discovers God's supreme domination over all creation, and the superior serves in the place of God. Revelation tells us that Christ established a hierarchy in His Church, and the superior is in the place of Christ. Ignatius goes on to describe three degrees of obedience, general and particular methods for acquiring perfect obedience (here he posits "blind" obedience which has since been a source of controversy), and some practical recommendations, the most significant of which, is that the ultimate motive for the virtue of obedience is the love of Christ, the great Model and Teacher of perfect obedience. Two notes are important here: the Christological character of obedience with the implication of supernatural assistance, with Ignatius' philosophical observation (in the Third Degree of obedience) that the internal conformity of mind with that of a superior can be had because it is possible for the will to direct the intellect; and this theological observation, that the will, in keeping the intellect from going astray, is aided by supernatural grace. This, as we are to see, is precisely what concerns Hopkins in his *Commentary*. Finally, the truly obedient state, the kind of courageous loyalty Ignatius esteemed, consists in the unity of the affections and desires with choice. This, he insisted, is the equanimity of soul that assures loyalty. This psychological insight into human nature is the basic perspective of the Spiritual Exercises, for Christ is put before the exercitant as supremely desirable, and the will is induced through prayer and grace to choose or elect Him.

The last central consideration for us in Hopkins' *Commentary* is his wrestling to express the stress of redemptive grace in the world and the instressing of it by man. In his scheme we have seen something of his thought about the constitution of nature in terms of creaturehood, and we have just examined his concepts of the role of Christ in creation. In a sense, we now turn back to nature to discover how divine grace is efficacious in creation, especially man, and how it relates to a nature that is free, as is human nature. In a word, how do person, grace, and free-will relate? This passage is one of the longest in the *Commentary,* written in relation to the General Examen of Conscience in the Spiritual Exercises. Though his thoughts probably arose at his consideration of this section of the Exercises, it is clear in his extensive speculation that he saw this to be precisely the crux of his own understanding as well as the crux of the Spiritual Exercises: the election of Christ as the living concrete norm of right order and perfection.

In the Second Week, Ignatius directs the consideration of the two meditations which confront the exercitant with two monumental choices. Knowing the sinfulness and weakness of his own person from the First Week, he is now called to decide whether he will elect to serve under one of two standards, Christ and His kingdom, or the principality of Satan. Moreover, in what degree of sacrifice to serve? With what kind of humility in what class of men will he serve? Ignatius' aim is no less than the knowledge and love of the person and doctrine of the Redeemer; and to follow Him, "to assimilate the life of Jesus Christ." The Third and Fourth Weeks are meditative exercises on the "great sacrifice" of Christ in order that the exercitant might strengthen his election of Christ to the point of a grand and total love.

Hopkins, then, was touching on the heart of the matter. It was really the point of it all. No reader should divorce these speculations from their biographical relationships. They come out of and go into the very life of Hopkins. They were the making and breaking points of his vocation and his artistry, "the strong/Spur, live and lancing" and "Time's eunuch."

Again Duns Scotus showed the way for Hopkins. Scotus is considered a voluntarist in a good sense, philosophically speaking. He taught ". . . that the intellect and the will together form the rational nature of man, but the will is the superior. The intellect is always determined by its object, but the will is free and is never restricted by the intellectual presentation of the good."[26] Scotus' point is, in his distinction between desire and choice, that while the power of rational love is irresistible, the power of choosing is not inundated, but retains its intrinsic power. Love is a free act. Hopkins' version makes a similar distinction between "elective will" and "affective will."

He begins his comment by defining the will: "By the will is meant that which decides action in us, *arbitrium,* or the faculty which is affected well or ill towards things, *voluntas.*"[27] He distinguishes three kinds of freedom, freedom of pitch, play and field: "This is the natural order of the three: freedom of pitch, that is, self-determination, is in the chooser himself and his choosing faculty; freedom of play is in the execution; freedom of field is in the object, the field of choice."[28] Thus freedom of pitch is choice, for "It is choice as when in English we say 'because I choose,' which means no more than (and with precision does mean) I instress my will to so-and-so. . . . And no freedom is more perfect . . . ."[29]

Hopkins, having already asserted that "A person is defined a rational (that is, intellectual) supposit," and that "A supposit is a self,"[30] states that freedom consists of a self and a rational nature: "It is the self then that supplies the determination, the difference, but the nature that supplies the exercise, and in these two things freedom consists."[31] Self, then, which has a rational nature possesses a pitch, a self-determination, or as Hopkins further describes it, "So also *pitch* is ultimately simple positiveness, that by which being differs from and is more than nothing and not-being, and it is with precision expressed by the English *do* (the simple auxiliary), which when we employ or emphasize, as 'he said it, he did say it,' we do not mean that the fact is any more a fact but that we the more state it. . . . So that this pitch might be expressed, if it were good English, *the doing* be, *the doing* choose, *the doing* so-and-so in that sense. Where there was no question of will it would become mere fact; where there is will it is free action, moral action. And such 'doing be,' and the thread or chain of such pitches or 'doing-be' 's, prior to nature's being overlaid, is self, personality. . . ."[32] Having stated the relation between self and pitch, he asks, "Is not this pitch or whatever we call it then the same as Scotus's *ecceitas* [sic]?"[33] Obviously, he thinks it is.

Free action is moral action. Moral action has two aspects, the act of consent and the commission: "We are then to distinguish, according to St. Ignatius (and I think Scotus has a distinction amounting to it), the act of commission and the act of consent. The first can never be guilty without the second, without, I mean, the second physically existing before, or with or at all events, after it (as in ratification, after-avowal) to give it guilt; but the first, the act of consent, may exist in all its guilt without the second."[34] On the other hand, good or meritorious action "is by simple dissent (consent inverted), . . . [or] by dissent from or disavowal of the commission which is then in some sort taking place in the subject himself in his own despite."[35] He notes that "guilt is primarily in the will and its consent, next in the commission or act forbidden."[36] Finally, Hopkins suggests a scale of moral action or freedom which is determined by the perfection of the rational nature: "Now if self begins to manifest its freedom with the rise from an irrational to a rational nature it is according to analogy to expect it will manifest more freedom with further rise in nature. Accordingly we find a more tremendous difference in fate between the good and fallen angels than between good and bad or even saved and lost men. And this reasoning is of wide application. But the scale of natures is infinite up towards the divine."[37] Thus an evil committed by an angel is more grievous than one committed by a man.

There are two points of consideration at this stage. First, recall that Ignatius' notion of obedience was the identification of desire and choice, that is, a union of the "elective will" and the "affective will," or the *arbitrium* and the *voluntas*, to bring in Hopkins. In his writings on obedience, Ignatius called this "obedience of the understanding," by which he meant, if I understand him, that the Ignatian man should love what he chooses, which is Christ. When choice and desire are at odds, he counseled diligent effort back toward their identification.

A second consideration is that both choice and desire go into the totality of an act of love. Students of Scotus make it clear that in his view there would be no act without their inter-reaction. Hopkins saw this relationship clearly. When there was perfect union of the two, there existed true love, a presage of heaven; when there was a seeming impossibility of their union, a hint of hell. A state of consolation was the normal state, a union of choice and desire. The prototypic cases are Lucifer before his fall and Christ in Gethsemane, the one resulting in an irremediable divorce and the other a sublime union.

Finally, looking at Hopkins' life and setting it against what he wrote in this regard, it seems at times that he felt an opposition in his soul between the heart and the head. This is particularly true of the last part of his life. One way of seeing this difficulty is his too great a reliance on Scotus, or a misunderstanding of Ignatian obedience, or the beginnings of mysticism. These points will be considered in the section on the late sonnets. They grow out of Hopkins' intense periods of disconsolation.

It is a prime concept of Ignatian discipline that man attaches himself to creatures as an end and thus what should be a means to his true end, God, becomes a means to spiritual death ultimately leading to damnation. In this case, man's free acts are willed with no regard for his last end. Because of his weakness, man is in imminent danger of having this happen. He needs help from above and God provides it. First, Hopkins notes that it is within God's powers: "God then can shift the self that lies in one to a higher, that is better, pitch of itself; that is, to a pitch or determination of itself on the side of good."[38] Moreover, "in every circumstance it is within God's power to determine the creature to choose, and freely choose, according to his will; but not without a change or access or circumstance, over and above the base act of determination on his part. The access is either of grace, which is 'super-nature,' to nature or of more grace to grace already given, and it takes the form of instressing the affective will."[39]

Now, it may be asked whether man's free will is a participator in any way when God sends his help or whether his free will action is hindered. Hopkins insists that man's will is not impaired; indeed, he must willingly accept God's grace. Hopkins' word for this willing acceptance is "correspondence": "For there must be something which shall be truly the creature's in the work of corresponding with grace: this is the *arbitrium*, the verdict on God's side, the saying Yes, the 'doing-agree' (to speak barbarously), and looked at in itself, such a nothing is the creature before its creator, it is found to be no more than the mere wish, discernible by God's eyes, that it might do as he wishes, might correspond, might say Yes to him; correspondence itself is on man's side not so much corresponding as the wish to correspond, and this least sigh of desire, this one aspiration, is the life and spirit of man."[40] Furthermore, he tells that correspondence is a grace itself, "For the momentary and constrained correspondence, being a momentary shift from a worse, ungracious, to a better, a gracious self, is a grace, a favour, and it is grace in the strict sense of that word; it is grace bestowed for the moment offered for a continuance."[41]

Hopkins also tells us that it is quite fitting that God should provide such assistance to man, for only He has unlimited vision:

> As besides the actual world there is an infinity of possible worlds, differing in all degrees of difference from what now is down to the having nothing in common with it but virgin matter, each of which possible worlds and this the actual one are like so many "cleaves" or exposed faces of some pomegranate (or other fruit) cut in all directions across: so there is an infinity of possible strains of action and choice for each possible self in these worlds (or, what comes to the same thing, in virgin matter) and the sum of these strains would be also like a pomegranate in the round, which God sees whole but of which we see at best only one cleave. Rather we see the world as one cleave and

the life of each person as one vein or strain of colour in it.[42]

Hopkins defines grace "as an action, activity, on God's part by which, in creating or after creating, he carries the creature to or towards the end of its being, which is its self-sacrifice to God and its salvation,"[43] and he distinguishes three kinds of grace: " (1) quickening, stimulating towards the object, towards good; this is especially in the affective will, might be a natural grace, and in a high degree seems to be the grace of novices; (2) corrective, turning the will from one direction or pitting into another, like the needle through an arc, determining its choice (I mean, stimulating that determination, which it still leaves free): this touches the elective will or the power of election and is especially the grace of a mature mind; (3) elevating, which lifts the receiver from one cleave of being to another and to a vital act in Christ: this is truly God's finger touching the very vein of personality, which nothing else can reach and man can respond to by no play whatever, by bare acknowledgement only, the counterstress which God alone can feel (*subito probas eum*), the aspiration in answer to his inspiration."[44]

He goes on to note those purposes for which God intended these kinds of graces. First, he remarks that man was created in grace, and had his will addressed towards his Creator. The grace here, he notes, was quickening grace. He also calls it creative grace, "the grace which destined the victim for the sacrifice, and which belongs to God the Father."[45] After the Fall, redeeming or corrective graces were provided through the restrictions of the Law, and the exhortations of the Prophets. More especially by Christ Himself. Hopkins remarks that the words of Christ "are either words of cure, as '*Veniam et curabo eum*,' '*Volo mundare*,' or corrections of some error or fault; their function is always *remener à la route*."[46] Christ's grace he sees as a purifying and mortifying grace "bringing the victim to the altar and sacrificing it."[47] When Christ ascended this grace was no longer bestowed and thus at Pentecost elevating grace was given to man to fasten him in good: "This is especially the grace of the Holy Ghost and is the acceptance and assumption of the victim of the sacrifice."[48] Hopkins follows this discussion of the purposes of these graces with quotations from scripture which are intended to reinforce his analysis.

The greatest event in man's history was the coming of Christ, for through the Incarnation man's dignity was not only restored to its former status, but elevated to a greater glory in the sight of God. It was Christ who became man's source of grace following his fall. In writing on grace Hopkins asserts that man becomes Christ through the action of grace: "It is, I say, any such activity on God's part; so that so far as this action or activity is God's it is divine stress, holy spirit, and all is done through Christ, Christ's spirit; so far as it is action, correspondence, on the creature's it is *actio salutaris;* so far as it is looked at in *esse quieto* it is Christ in his member on the one side, his member in Christ on the other. It is as if a man said: That is Christ playing at me and me playing at Christ, only that it is no play but truth; that is Christ *being me* and me being Christ."[49] It is important to notice that his view of grace is quite in keeping with the Ignatian spirit, for it preserves the Christo-centric aspect of the Spiritual Exercises with Christ as king, exemplar, and redeemer. The eminent, modern commentator on the Exercises, Father Hugo Rahner, in emphasizing the centrality of Christ in the Exercises, wrote ". . . why and for what end we were created we can learn only from Christ our Lord. . . ."[50]

The correspondency is significant. The "quickening" grace pertains to Ignatius' statement of creation and all that follows from it (the Principle and Foundation): God created man in this grace which destined him for loving sacrifice. But man did not properly correspond and was taken out of this state of grace. Through Christ he was restored to grace, this time, "corrective" grace. This is the grace of purification through sacrifice with Christ as model and exemplar. This pertains especially to the two Examens of Conscience and specifically to the Incarnate Christ of the Second Week, the Passionate Christ of the Third Week, and the Risen Christ of the Fourth Week. Man's correspondence to this grace is to be Christ. Hopkins put it clearly in a comment on Ignatius' First Contemplation of the Third Week (on the Last Supper, here the fourth point): "These three points are (1) Christ's human nature and how it suffered: the victim; (2) his godhead and how (A) it spares or lets do, (B) forsakes and lets donate: the priest or giver of the victim; (3) me, the culprit, the lost sheep, the redeemed. Then further we are (1) to suffer with Christ suffering, (2) keep sight of the godhead hiding, (3) repay if we can the price of our redemption."[51] The third grace, "elevating" grace, is the inspiring grace of the Holy Spirit which lifts man up to a level of sacrificial love that becomes, as Hopkins put it, "a vital act in Christ." This grace relates to the final contemplation of the Exercises, the Contemplation for Obtaining Love, which is their ultimate goal. Hopkins stated this in a short comment on this contemplation. It ends with the following remark which is a fitting final touch for both his and Ignatius' vision: "And God *in forma servi* rests *in servo*, that is, Christ as a solid in his member as a hollow or shell, both things being the image of God; which can only be perfectly when the member is in all things conformed to Christ. This too best brings out the nature of the man himself, as the lettering on a sail or device upon a flag are best seen when it fills."[52] The essence of this last exercise of the Spiritual Exercises is an "uninterrupted act of love" through "uninterrupted service." As Hopkins put it in the *Commentary*, "repay if we can," in his poetry, "Give beauty back. . . ." This final disposition of his thought, developed over a lifetime, meaningfully integrates with the novice master of his soul, St. Ignatius, through the heritage of his Spiritual Exercises. What started as the stress of being through inscape became for him the stress of grace through Christ-scape. The object? That beauty not die. The Ignatian way: "His mystery must be instressed, stressed. . . ."

The final shape of Hopkins' vision was Ignatian.

CHAPTER THREE

Ignatius and the Wreck

"Thou heardst me truer than tongue confess
Thy terror, O Christ, O God."

Perhaps no other trait was more emphasized by Ignatius
than the Jesuit's need for prudent and discreet love, and this
cannot be accomplished without discerning the darkness of
Belial from that of the light of Christ. The Rules for the
Discernment of Spirits are really means to distinguish the graces
of God from the wiles of the devil written by Ignatius for his
Company and based on his own experiences during his conversion after Pamplona and his retreat at Manresa. Ignatius
knew that the battle would never be waged against Satan
effectively unless the Jesuit soldier always knew what was truly
God's issue in the foray. These Rules are crucial to the efficacy
of the Spiritual Exercises, for the exercitant must prayerfully
learn the relationships existing between nature and grace, between the world and Christ. This basic knowledge is vital to
the discreet and prudent service of the man who has elected
to serve in the army of Christ, for this service involves an entire
renunciation of the world and a pledge to wrest the world from
Satan by commingling with the world. When Ignatius drew up
the qualifications for a general of the Order in the Constitutions
(IX, 2, 6), he stressed heavily discretion and prudence in all
those matters pertaining to the interior life and the management
of men. The soldier of Christ must ever be on his guard to
discern the mysterious actions of God in the affairs of men.
Hopkins was learning this at St. Beuno's in his training as a
Jesuit when he wrote his longest, most imposing poem, in which

he poetically expresses his discernment of the mysterious ways of God in the affairs of man.

In a letter to R. W. Dixon, Hopkins recorded the circumstances of the writing of *The Wreck of the Deutschland*:

> What I had written I burnt before I became a Jesuit and resolved to write no more, as not belonging to my profession, unless it were by the wish of my superiors; so for seven years I wrote nothing but two or three little presentation pieces which occasion called for. But when in the winter of '75 the Deutschland was wrecked in the mouth of the Thames and five Franciscan nuns, exiles from Germany by the Falck Laws, aboard her were drowned I was affected by the account and happening to say so to my rector he said that he wished someone would write a poem on the subject. On this hint I set to work and, though my hand was out at first, produced one. I had long had haunting my ear the echo of a new rhythm which now I realised on paper.[1]

Two things are significant here. The first is the complete commitment with which Hopkins entered the Society of Jesus. He burned all of his poems; he did not write again until prompted by his superior. This is no small abnegation for a man of Hopkins' creative inclinations. Though our knowledge of his personal life after he entered the Order in 1868 is not voluminous, nevertheless the Journal he kept from this time until February of 1875 has a number of entries that indicate that Hopkins was undergoing an Ignatian change. For example, there is a passage which describes his impression of Wales and his intention to learn Welsh. Using the Spiritual Exercises as a guide, he decided that he should refrain, for his intentions were what Ignatius would call inordinate. Hopkins began altering his intentions, but Ignatius had the last word: ". . . I had not sooner given up the Welsh than my desire seemed to be for the conversion of Wales and I had it in mind to give everything else for that; nevertheless weighing this by St. Ignatius' rules of election I decided not to do so."[2]

Apparently Hopkins kept two Journals simultaneously, one given to nonreligious notations and the other to religious ones. Only the former is extant.[3] This being the case it is significant how often his religious life creeps into the notes in his non-religious Journal, notes that indicate that he was undergoing a metamorphosis that was fundamentally changing his whole life. This is especially clear in his jottings of nature impressions which often have a religious turn of one kind or another, such as his entry, "Feb. 5 and 6 were almost hot. Daffodils have been in bloom for some days. A weeping willow here is all green. The elms have long been in red bloom and yesterday (the 11th) I saw small leaves on the brushwood at their roots. Some primroses out. But a penance which I was doing from Jan. 25 to July 25 prevented my seeing much that half-year."[4] In another entry of September 24, 1870 (he took his first vows on the eighth) he describes in detail his impression of the Northern Lights. He closed the entry with the following: "This busy working of nature wholly independent of the earth and seeming to go on in a strain of time not reckoned by our reckoning of days and years but simpler and as if correcting the preoccupation of the world by being preoccupied with and appealing to and dated to the day of judgment was like a new witness to God and filled me with delightful fear."[5] On October 20 of the same year he entered a close description of the river near him. The entry begins, "Oct. 20—Laus Deo—the river today and yesterday."[6] And so on throughout the extant Journals, the Ignatian discipline began taking root in Hopkins' being, and surfacing itself in his daily jottings.

In 1874 Hopkins began reading theology at St. Beuno's College in North Wales. He was beginning the last step to the Jesuit priesthood. By now the Ignatian discipline had transformed him, and no one was so aware of the change as was Hopkins himself. When his superior prompted him to write something about the wreck of the Deutschland, Hopkins was still close enough to his own "wreck" that when he set out to write on the Deutschland, he could not help seeing a profound parallel between the Kentish Knock and the Spiritual

Exercises.[7] It is notable that his "wreck" forms the first part of the poem.

Mr. F. R. Leavis wrote of this first work, "This poem was his first ambitious experiment, and it is the more interesting in that his technical resources are deployed in it at great length: the association of inner, spiritual, emotional stress with physical reverberations, nervous and muscular tensions that characterize his best verse is here explicitly elaborated in an account of the storm which is at the same time an account of an inner drama. The wreck he describes is both occasion and symbol."[8] This is an accurate general statement about the poem, but it by no means conveys the specific structure of the poem. Mr. Leavis tells us that Hopkins vividly realizes that the wreck is in him and at the same time that he is in it. He notes that Hopkins views the actual wreck as an example of the sort of "worldly disaster that brings conviction, supernatural assurance to the soul . . . and identifies such experience mystically with Christ's passion."[9] While there is no question of the general validity of these observations, Mr. Leavis has left much to be said about the poem.

There are two parallel wrecks in the poem. Both force dire spiritual and physical consequences on the stranded. Both cause anguish and suffering analogous to the Passion. Both are providential in that each must make an "election" regarding his salvation. Both end in God's mastery. Part the First deals with Hopkins' own wreck on *The Spiritual Exercises;* Part the Second deals with the nuns' plight in the wreck of the Deutschland (including the plight, of course, of all those on the ship).

The first wreck explains why the first part of the poem is so entirely subjective, and it helps explain why Hopkins intrudes himself into the second part of the poem. It is no wonder he could write to Robert Bridges concerning the poem: "I may add for your greater interest and edification that what refers to myself in the poem is all strictly and literally true and all did occur; nothing is added for poetical padding."[10] Hopkins views the two wrecks as identical in their essential spiritual implications: God desires to master his creature while yet respecting his nature, to do this He employs "quickening" graces, "corrective" graces, and "elevating" graces to assist man's darkened intellect and enfeebled will to elect Him Master. These graces may involve a "crash" or a "lingering-out sweet skill." The two wrecks are of the nature of a crash through the not so obvious instrument of the stress of divine grace. The poem is about a man and a woman who read rightly the news that the world brings, the Word, Christ, and how both of them instressed the stress of God upon them thereby offering to God the re-enactment of the Incarnation and Redemption as other Christs. Hopkins stated in this way in his *Commentary*: "The world, man, should after its own manner give God being in return for that being he has given. This is done by the great sacrifice. To contribute then to that sacrifice is the end for which man was made."[11]

The first part of the poem, then, can be taken as a description of Hopkins' own experiencing of the Spiritual Exercises. So viewed, it is also a poetic statement of their spiritual implications. Of course, there are allusions which can be taken as explicit and implicit references to all the Four Weeks of the Exercises. The first stanza opens with a statement of the theme of the entire poem, "Thou mastering me/God!" which Hopkins weaves in symphonic fashion throughout the poem. It is the *leit motif* of the whole work. This is followed with an elaboration of the basic axiom, God as Creator of all. Hopkins has in effect simply stated in poetic mode the first principle of the Foundation of the Exercises, that man was created to serve God. He notes that the nature God gave to man "almost unmade" him, that is, God gave man a free will which in abuse caused rebellion and exile that resulted in such a degeneration of his nature that it almost destroyed him. Hopkins is here expressing the devastation of Original Sin. He echoes Blake, "what with dread / Thy doing." Now he asks whether he, fallen man, is being renovated: "and dost thou touch me afresh?" The final line of the stanza is a perception of God's sustaining finger in his being which stresses upon him his origin and his destiny. It is an allusion to the three modes of grace, the last of which he set forth in his *Commentary*:[12]

"elevating, which lifts the receiver from one cleave of being to another and to a vital act in Christ: this is truly God's finger touching the very vein of personality, which nothing else can reach and man can respond to by no play whatever, by bare acknowledgement only, the counterstress which God alone can feel (*'subito probas eum'*), the aspiration in answer to his inspiration."[13]

In his own case, he tells us in stanza 2, there was "acknowledgement." Amidst the spiritual storm brought on by the self-scrutiny of the First Week of the Exercises, the truths of the Foundation came hurtling down on his rebellious egoistic nature. The Ignatian assessment of his existence in all its frightening implications is expressed in stanza 2. Under the pressures of this "quickening" grace, the First Week of the Exercises, Hopkins corresponded: "I did say yes/O at lightning and lashed rod," which is "corrective" grace of the Second Week. This whole stanza can be taken as a reference to his novitiate and the impact of the Exercises upon him. The allusion, "walls, altar and hour and night," is quite probably a reference to the circumstances involved in the making of the Exercises. Furthermore, there is no more accurate description of the First Week of the Exercises than "Trod/Hard down with a horror of height," for this is precisely the psychological effect of the First Week. The exercitant, having realized the implications of his creation (Foundation), reflects on his sins, his past disorder. He sees himself "as an ulcer and abscess whence have issued so many sins and so many iniquities, and such vile poison." A "horror of height" indeed. Ignatius says, "Consider who God is, against Whom I have sinned, looking at His attributes, comparing them with their contraries in myself: His wisdom with my ignorance, His omnipotence with my weakness, His justice with my iniquity, His goodness with my malice."[14] He asks how is it the earth "has not opened to swallow me up, creating new hells that I might suffer in them forever."[15] It is not surprising that Hopkins expresses the afflictive forces of grace let loose on him through the Exercises in terms of physical suffering: "And the midriff astrain with leaning of, laced with fire of stress."

In the third stanza, Hopkins sees himself trapped on the one side by his sins and the horror they lead to, and on the other, he is confronted by his Master against Whom he has offended: "where was a place?" This is the frantic dilemma in which Ignatius puts the exercitant during the First Week: the frown before and the hurtle after. The meditations on personal sin and Hell during this Week enforce on him the terrible consequences of his being. In the powerful guidance of Ignatius, he "flings" himself, delivers his heart "to the heart of the Host."[16] He envisions his "carrier-witted" soul ("carrier-witted" because God is its home) passing through the three stages of Christian perfection, the Purgative, the Illuminative, and the Unitive, "from the flame to the flame then, tower from the grace to the grace." That this spiritual way is progressive and perfective is clear from the transition from the first verb "flash" to the final one "tower." Hopkins has in effect envisioned the three remaining Weeks of the Exercises by tele-scoping their progressive steps (the Exercises, of course, have incorporated in them these three stages) into one poetic line. That the line is vague serves only to emphasize that Hopkins was attempting to describe the ineffable experiences involved in obtaining perfect love of God, the last contemplation, it will be recalled, of the Exercises.

Moreover, this "fling of the heart" is the high point of the first part of the poem. It is "the aspiration in answer to his inspiration." It is Ignatius' *senalarse mas en servicio.* It is the "Election" of the Exercises. Hopkins' correspondence, his "fling" is just the effect that the First and Second Weeks of the Exer-cises intend. As he put it in his *Commentary:* "For there must be something which shall be truly the creature's in the work of corresponding with grace: this is the *arbitrium,* the verdict on God's side, the saying Yes, the 'doing-agree' (to speak barbarously), and looked at in itself, such a nothing is the creature before its creator, it is found to be no more than the mere wish, discernible by God's eyes, that it might do as he wishes, might correspond, might say Yes to him."[17]

After having considered the way of Christian perfection, Hopkins turns in the fourth stanza to examine his human status, his physical life. He employs the metaphor of an hour-glass, the glass signifying life, the sand his physical being. The sand "at the wall / Fast," suggests the seeming permanence of his life, but life is "mined with a motion, a drift," which suggests the steady dissolution of physical life until it completely gives way, that is, "to the fall." Then the image changes to that of pooled water which has gathered at the base of the uplands. The welled water is fed by the drops of water trickling down the side of the mountain. The meaning is that man's spiritual life (the well) is sustained by the message in the gospel of the Incarnate Christ whose love (grace) feeds (trickles into) man's spiritual life. In juxtaposing these two images, Hopkins has tersely stated the dichotomy that man represents in his makeup of body and soul. Further, he expressed the same idea of God's grace assisting man's spiritual life in his *Commentary*: "Nevertheless in every circumstance it is within God's power to determine the creature to choose, and freely choose, according to his will; but not without a change or access of circumstance. . . . This access is either of grace, which is 'super-nature,' to nature or of more grace to grace already given, and it takes the form of instressing the affective will, of affecting the will towards the good which he proposes."[18]

In stanza 5 Hopkins turns to another means of knowing God,[19] that revelation that comes through immediate contact with Nature: "I kiss my hand / To the stars, lovely-asunder / Starlight, wafting him out of it." The whole concept of created things leading man back to the Creator of them is in the Foundation of the Exercises: "The other things on the face of the earth were created for man's sake, and in order to aid him in the prosecution of the end for which he was created."[20] Ignatius saw this as such an important means in man's salvation that he incorporated two principles in the Foundation which are peculiarly Ignatian, the principle of proper use of creatures and the principle of indifference. The importance Ignatius gave these two principles is evident by the fact they were laid down in the Foundation of the Exercises as conclusions that must follow from God's purpose in creating man and all other things. As noted previously, Ignatius believed that the reason men frustrate their being is their inordinate relationship with created things. The Spiritual Exercises were written primarily that man be enabled to remove all such inordinate attachment.

The last three lines of the stanza emphasize the sacramental aspect of Nature. Again Hopkins employs two characteristic terms, instress and stress (which have already been discussed). Whenever he uses these specialized names, especially in poetry, they are freighted with meanings. They may be taken in the ordinary sense of "to emphasize," but if some of Hopkins' own meanings are applied, the whole stanza is markedly enriched. In this case, Hopkins would be saying that God's mystery must have its unique nature brought out, that is, to employ Scholastic terminology of act and perfection, God's mystery must be brought by man into "act," into soul reality (it actually exists, but not all men know it). According to Scholastics, in the epistemological activity on the part of the knower, there is a transition from potency to act, that is, there is an "actualization" in which the unique individuality of the mystery is directly (Thomas Aquinas would say indirectly or reflexively; Hopkins was a Scotist in this matter) known by man. On the part of the thing knowable, its distinct individuality (Hopkins called it pitch) "stresses" itself, that is, its intrinsic potency, which Hopkins called passive power, to be known. It is in this latter use that he employs the term in the last line of the second stanza: it is the passive power of God's mystery actualizing in him that laced him with fire. Both are employed in stanza 5. God's mystery must be "realized" by man in all things; its full nature must be brought out. That Hopkins used these terms in his own senses of them is borne out by his reference to knowing in the last line of the stanza: "for I greet him the days I meet him, and bless when I understand." The other key word is, "bless," for to know of God's mystery is a blessed understanding.

In the sixth stanza, Hopkins tells us that the stress of Christ's sacrificial mystery "rides time like riding a river." It is in creation. It is through Nature that God stresses on us His mystery. In his *Commentary* he wrote: "The power therefore of going on from worse to better depends on the outward grace of God's ordinary providence, which brings fresh natural motives day by day before us and in the course of time, in growing from childhood to manhood and youth to age, on the whole stronger ones."[21]

God entered time at the Incarnation, Hopkins tells us in stanza 7, and this dates the mysteries of Christianity. He notes in reviewing the mysteries of Christ from Bethlehem to Calvary that man instresses them only when he is "wrecked," "only the heart, being hard at bay, / Is out with it!" Then like a ripe sloe bursting in the mouth when it is squashed (Shakespeare would have liked this figure) so Christ's mysteries are actualized "Brim, in a flash, full!" in men's driven hearts and they rush "To the hero of Calvary, Christ's feet." Sometimes it happens early in life, sometimes late. And Hopkins tells us they do it in spite of meaning, wish, or warning. In his *Commentary* he put it: "It is into that possible world that God for the moment moves his creature out of this one or it is from that possible world he brings his creature into this, shewing it to itself gracious and consenting; nay more, clothing its old self for the moment with a gracious and consenting self. This shift is grace. For grace is any action, activity, on God's part by which, in creating or after creating, he carries the creature to or towards the end of its being, which is its selfsacrifice to God and its salvation. It is, I say, any such activity on God's part; so that so far as this action or activity is God's it is divine stress, holy spirit, and, as all is done through Christ, Christ's spirit."[22] It will be recalled that the Second Week of the Exercises is spent meditating on the mysteries of Christ's hidden life and His public life, and that the Third Week is an intense contemplation of the Passion.

Stanzas 9 and 10 correspond to the Fourth Week of the Exercises especially the Contemplation of Perfect Love. Like the exercitant colloquizing with the Risen Saviour, in stanza 9 Hopkins prays to obtain perfect love of God. Expressing the paradox which is at the very heart of Christianity, Good Friday and Easter Sunday, he asks the Lord to send men their Good Fridays so that they shall have their Easter Sundays: "Beyond saying sweet, past telling of tongue, / Thou art lightning and love, I found it, a winter and warm; Father and fondler of heart thou hast wrung: / Hast thy dark descending and most art merciful then." The crucial expression is, "I found it." This again points up the intensely personal aspect of the first part of the poem. In stanza 10 he describes two of the "possible worlds" into which God had moved men which brought them to Him, the one, like Paul, which with flame and fire, "at a crash," forged God's will in him, and the other, like St. Augustine, which silently instills through a period of time the will of the Lord, a melting that comes as a result of "a lingering-out sweet skill." The last lines represent a poetic version of the Ignatian Contemplation of Divine Love as well as a recapitulation in a symphonic sense of the basic theme: "Make mercy in all of us, out of us all / Mastery, but be adored, but be adored King."

In the second half of the poem, Hopkins turns to the other wreck, the other "crash." Perhaps before looking at the section in detail, it will be well to recall some of the historical facts concerning the incident.[23] The Deutschland, owned by the North German Lloyd Company, set sail for New York on Sunday morning, December 5, 1875. Though the ship's papers were lost, the ship's commander, a Captain Brickenstein, testified that "there were about 107 emigrants with other passengers, and 99 crew."[24] The weather was heavy. About five o'clock Monday morning, her screw having been broken, she struck the sands of the Kentish Knock. She lay there helpless until ten o'clock Tuesday morning when a Liverpool tugboat out of Harwich came and took off all who were alive, 138 people. During this time, according to witnesses, many boats passed by, but they did not respond to her distress signals. During an inquest, it was brought out that the distress signals sent up on Monday night were seen in Harwich, but nothing was done about it even though there were plenty of sailors available. It was made clear that a good many of them did not wish to risk their lives in such bad weather. However, the main excuse offered for the inactivity was that there was no lifeboat at Harwich (it was also said that the need for one was often felt in Harwich).

The wreck was widely publicized. The newspapers were loud in their condemnation of the people of Harwich who left to her fate a distressed ship stranded off the English coast for thirty hours. Moreover, those that did come considered her a derelict and ransacked her.

The majority of the deaths took place early Tuesday morning. The passengers, who had remained for the most part calm, were ordered out of their cabins. Most of them obeyed. On deck they clustered on the wheelhouse and on the tops of other structures. Many of the crew and some passengers went into the rigging where they were safe as long as they could hold on. The ship had become waterlogged from the rising tide. The intense cold and exposure were too much. Some of those on the rigging lost their holds and fell into the sea. Men, women, and children were swept away from their shelters on deck into the sea. Some tried to commit suicide. One man succeeded in hanging himself behind the wheelhouse. The tide did not abate until about eight o'clock. Then the survivors were able to go safely on deck. Among those lost were five nuns of the Franciscan order. They were from a convent in Westphalia, having been exiled from their native land because of the Falk Laws.

In stanza 11, Hopkins personifies Death marching through humanity in triumph. Yet man remains complacent, even though he sees death everywhere. Man forgets "that there must/The sour scythe cringe, and the blear share come." It is with this shortsightedness of their fate that he pictures in stanza 12 the humanity which "On Saturday sailed from Bremen, / American-outward-bound." He notes that a fourth of the two hundred souls aboard were to be drowned, and he asks of the Lord whether it meant a harvest of souls for Him: "Yet did the dark side of the bay of thy blessing / Not vault them, the millions of rounds of thy mercy not reeve even them in?" Certainly, he is saying, it was in God's providence that "The goal was a shoal, of a fourth the doom to be drowned."

In stanzas 13, 14, and 15, Hopkins describes the actual wreck. He followed the newspaper accounts of it very closely, in places almost word for word. Critics of the poem have not made much of its descriptive quality. When one reads through some of the

contemporary newspaper accounts and becomes aware of how
closely Hopkins followed them, one cannot help being struck
by the sheer descriptive power with which he painted the
tragedy. He never once lapses into prosaic, and though the
poem has considerable ideality, he never lets it make inroads
on his realistic treatment. Moreover, he combines the ideality
and the realism with extraordinary success: "Wiry and white-
fiery and whirlwind-swivelled snow / Spins to the widow-making
unchilding unfathering deeps."

Stanza 16 provides an instance for study of Hopkins' creative
powers, for it is wholly given over to his poetic handling of
one of the incidents he read in a newspaper account: "One
brave sailor, who was safe in the rigging, went down to try and
save a child or woman who was drowning on deck. He was se-
cured by a rope to the rigging, but a wave dashed him against
the bulwarks, and when daylight dawned his headless body,
detained by the rope, was swaying to and fro with the waves."[25]
Using this brief report, Hopkins poetically realized it in every
detail making it dramatically effective through his management
of heightened language:

> One stirred from the rigging to save
> The wild woman-kind below,
> With a rope's end round the man, handy and brave—
> He was pitched to his death at a blow,
> For all his dreadnought breast and braids of thew:
> They could tell him for hours, dangled the to and fro
> Through the cobbled foam-fleece, what could he do
> With the burl of the fountains of air, buck and the flood of the
> wave.

In stanza 17, Hopkins, still following the newspaper accounts
in detail, introduces another incident which was vividly described, one which he made central in the second part of the
poem. This is the incident of the Franciscan nun who called
to God in the midst of the suffering and the dying until she
herself died.

Night roared, with the heart-break hearing a heart-broke
  rabble,
The woman's wailing, the crying of child without check—
  Till a lioness arose breasting the babble,
A prophetess towered in the tumult, a virginal tongue told.

Then in stanza 18, the poet intrudes himself at this moment
of spiritual crisis in his poem. He feels an intense bond with her:

Ah, touched in your bower of bone
  Are you! turned for an exquisite smart,
Have you! make words break from me here all alone,
  Do you! —mother of being in me, heart.

The whole thing somehow seems joyful to him. He asks,

What can it be, this glee? the good you have there
  of your own?

In stanza 19, he states why he feels her plight, her action,
her words so intensely. He had gone through the same thing.
God had him at bay just as He has her now. And he flung his
heart to the Host just as she is doing. It was because this was a

Sister, a sister callling
  A master, her master and mine!—
And the inboard seas run swirling and hawling;
  The rash smart sloggering brine
Blinds her; but she that weather sees one thing, one;
Has one fetch in her: she rears herself to divine
  Ears, and the call of the tall nun
To the men in the tops and the tackle rode over the storm's
  brawling.

All of this the poet got from a short passage in a newspaper
account: "One, noted for her extreme tallness, is the lady who,
at midnight on Monday, by standing on a table in the saloon,
was able to thrust her body through the skylight, and kept
exclaiming in a voice heard by those in the rigging above the

roar of the storm, 'My God, my God, make haste, make haste.' "[26]

In stanzas 20 to 23 (exclusive), the poet provides background regarding the nuns. However, stanza 20 is mostly a parenthesis, possibly as notable as Milton's intrusion in "Lycidas," in which Hopkins expresses some of the ironic complications he perceived in the name, "Deutschland." He notes that though it is known "world wide of its good," it connotes at least two "desperate" meanings, this shipwreck with its exiled emigrants and the heretical Martin Luther. This leads the poet to note a further irony. St. Gertrude, German mystical saint, and Luther both resided in the same town (Eisleben), and were mothered by the same church, yet the one is "Christ's lily," and the other the "beast of the waste wood." This brings a final reflection. The difference in offspring can be seen from the beginning, Cain and Abel, for example. Here is the passage:

(O Deutschland, double a desperate name!
    O world wide of its good!
But Gertrude, lily, and Luther, are two of a town,
Christ's lily and beast of the waste wood:
        From life's dawn it is drawn down
Abel is Cain's brother and breasts they have sucked the same.)

In stanza 21, Hopkins makes reference to the exile under the Falk Laws of the five nuns, resulting in their being aboard the *Deutschland* and in the wreck: "Thames would ruin them; / Surf, snow, river and earth / Gnashed." But Hopkins exclaims that all things happen under the providence of God, all things issue from His hands, especially, he felt, graces which bring men to Him. Here the poet dramatizes God's stroke: "but thou art above, thou Orion of light; / Thy unchancelling poising palms were weighing the worth, / Thou martyr-master: in thy sight / Storm flakes were scroll-leaved flowers, lily showers— sweet / Heaven was astrew in them." God makes martyrs of us in imitation of His passion so that we shall have, like Him, an eastering. The storm, then, indicative of God's will, was in His providence a shower of lilies. The five nuns were to have their Resurrection.

But before the crown comes the cross. In stanza 22, the poet recalling that their number was five sees this as a special sign of Christ's love. For this is the mystical number, His sacred sign, and all who follow Him must carry their crosses and be marked by His badge. Hopkins here makes a remarkable poetic reflection on the sacred wounds:

> Five! the finding and sake
> And cipher of suffering Christ.
> Mark, the mark is of man's make
> And the word of it Sacrificed.
> But he scores it in scarlet himself on his own bespoken,
> Before-time-taken, dearest prized and priced—
> Stigma, signal, cinquefoil token
> For lettering of lambs fleece, ruddying of the rose-flake.

The five were Franciscan nuns. St. Francis bore on his body the marks that men gave to Christ and he bore them, like Christ, in joy: "Joy fall to thee, father Francis, / Drawn to the Life that died; / With the gnarls of the nails in thee, niche of the lance, his / Lovescape crucified / And seal of his seraph-arrival." So His five spiritual daughters have received their "seal of his seraph-arrival," "Are sisterly sealed in wild waters / To bathe in his fall-gold mercies, to breathe in his all-fire glances."

In stanza 25, again the poet intrudes. He reflects on his own safety while the nuns were "the prey of the gales." He again enacts the high point of the poem, the suffering and death, the nun calling above the din to Christ: "She to the black-about air, to the breaker, the thickly / Falling flakes, to the throng that catches and quails / Was calling 'O Christ, Christ, come quickly': / The cross to her she calls Christ to her, christens her wild-worst Best." One of the newspaper accounts had these very words: "Five German nuns, whose bodies are now in the dead-house here, clasped hands and were drowned together, the chief sister, a gaunt woman 6 ft. high, calling out loudly and often 'Oh Christ, come quickly!' till the end came."[27]

The poet having reflected on the passion of these nuns with all of its spiritual implication, turns in the next three stanzas

(25-27) to consider their motives. When that tall nun called out to Christ, the poet asks, "what did she mean?" Was it, he asks, that she was aware that she was suffering as Christ did, "as her lover had been?" He recalls that the fearful apostles who awoke Christ on Lake Gennesaret certainly were not moved in the same way: "They were else-minded then." Or did she call for relief because of "the combating keen?" What is it, the poet asks, that causes the human heart in spite of all difficulties to hopefully aspire to its heart's desire? Maybe it is that the human heart is rooted in Paradise and always and ever it harkens back to that original abode. Hopkins presents through his beautiful imagery a vision of Paradise:

> For how to the heart's cheering
> The down-dugged ground-hugged grey
> Hovers off, the jay-blue heavens appearing
> Of pied and peeled May!
> Blue-beating and hoary-glow height; or night, still higher,
> With belled fire and the moth-soft Milky Way.

But this is a vision in hope. And every man has a different vision:

> What by your measure is the heaven of desire,
> The treasure never eyesight got, nor was ever guessed what for
> the hearing?

The poet answers, in his analysis of her motives, that she was not moved by danger, "electrical horror," nor by the fact that her plight is Passion-like, for "it finds / The appealing of the Passion is tenderer in prayer apart." He surmises that under the circumstances there were probably many things in "her mind's / Burden, in wind's burly and beat of endragoned seas." However, he affirms that it is restless, quenchless life that moved her, "The jading and jar of the cart, / Times tasking, it is fathers that asking for ease / Of the sodden-with-its-sorrowing heart."

Stanzas 28 through 30 are a poetic exaltation of what Hop-

kins saw as the operation of divine grace. In 28, the poet mani-
fests in his frenzied verse, not the distress of the wreck, but
the shock of the presence of the Lord, an event beyond the
descriptive capabilities of language: "Strike you the sight of
it? look at it loom there, / Thing that she . . . there then! the
Master, / Ipse, the only one, Christ, King, Head." In 29, the
poet continues his exaltation, only here it is of the tall nun
(symbolizing all five) who corresponded to God's grace: "Ah!
there was a heart right! / There was single eye! / Read the un-
shapeable shock night / And knew the who and the why." Knew
what? Knew what Ignatius wrote in the cave at Manresa, that
God's stress in all things leads man back to Him: "Wording it
how but by him that present and past, / Heaven and earth are
word of, worded by?" In his *Commentary* Hopkins wrote: "God's
utterance of himself in himself is God the Word, outside himself is this world. This world then is word, expression, news, of
God. Therefore its end, its purpose, its purport, its meaning, is
God, and its life or work to name and praise him."[28]

In the last line of stanza 28, the poet identifies the action
of the nun as Christ's action: "Let him ride, her pride, in his
triumph, despatch and have done with his doom there." In
stanza 30 he again expressed the same idea except here he sees
the nun as another Virgin Mary[29] conceiving Christ anew,
another Incarnation: "For so conceived, so to conceive thee is
done; / But here was heart-throe, birth of a brain, / Word, that
heard and kept thee and uttered thee outright." This identity
of Divine and human action is the mode of operation of
Divine grace as Hopkins understood it. The key to these passages of the poem was clearly expressed in his *Commentary*.
Having discussed the nature of free will of man, he turns to the
operation of grace:

> For grace is any action, activity, on God's part by which,
> in creating or after creating, he carries the creature to
> or towards the end of its being, which is its selfsacri-
> fice to God and its salvation. It is, I say, any such
> activity on God's part; so that so far as this action or

activity is God's it is divine stress, holy spirit, and,
as all is done through Christ, Christ's spirit; so far as
it is action, correspondence, on the creature's it is
actio salutaris; so far as it is looked at *in esse quieto*
it is Christ in his member on the one side, his member
in Christ on the other. It is as if a man said: That is
Christ playing at me and me playing at Christ, only
that it is no play but truth; That is Christ *being me*
and me being Christ.[30]

He expressed the same idea in his sonnet, "As kingfishers catch
fire." In the sestet he wrote that the just man,

Keeps grace: that keeps all his goings graces;
Acts in God's eye what in God's eye he is—
Christ—for Christ plays in ten thousand places,
Lovely in limbs, and lovely in eyes not his
To the Father through the features of men's faces.[31]

In stanza 31, the poet turns to the rest of the souls lost in
the wreck. The priest-poet laments them: "but pity the rest
of them! / Heart, go and bleed at a bitterer vein for the /
Comfortless unconfessed of them—." But relying on God's good
providence he visualizes the nun in a different role. He envisions
this "Simon Peter of a soul" as a "blown beacon of light" showing the way to these frightened souls, the way to salvation: "No
not uncomforted: lovely-felicitous Providence / Finger of a
tender of, O of a feathery delicacy, the breast of the / Maiden
could obey so, be a bell to, ring of it, and / Startle the poor
sheep back! is the shipwreck then a harvest,/Does tempest
carry a grain for thee?"

The last four stanzas are an ecstatic and sublime hymn of
praise to God in which the poet employs poetic language with
the magnitude and elevation of fully orchestrated sound in a
coda of a great symphonic piece. In another sense, it is an inspired poetic version of the Ignatian Contemplation for obtaining Divine Love which climaxes the Spiritual Exercises. It is a
kind of litany of the Divine in which the poet names the at-

tributes of God, enumerates the guises of His mercies, and then entreats His grace. The last stanza gives a remembrance to the "Dame, at our door / Drowned," asks that the Faith return to "rare-dear Britain," and ends in a finale of pounding expletives which proclaim the majesty of Christ the King: "Pride, rose, prince, hero of us, high-priest, / Our hearts' charity's hearth's fire, our thoughts' chivalry's throng's Lord."

There are two qualities in this poem that make it especially Ignatian. The first is that Hopkins in true Ignatian fashion discerns the action of God in this affair. He sees in the jeopardy of the wreck God placing men in such dire stress that they must choose, and choose quickly, to offer their lives to Him, again renewing The Passion and Death of Christ, made rich in eternal value by virtue of this commemoration. The other Ignatian quality that is notable is the kind of service to Christ that the five nuns offer. They give themselves over completely and irrevocably amid the most frightening circumstances. But it is not only that they commit themselves fully to Christ; it is also the way they do it. The way is heroic, chivalric, knightly. This is precisely the stamp that the soldierly Ignatius put on the Society of Jesus: the greatest sacrifice in the greatest danger made with the greatest generosity. These nuns fought under the standard of Christ to further the kingdom of Christ, and they did it with qualities of Christian knighthood. In doing so, they proclaimed in chivalric fashion the majesty of Christ the King, which is on its most profound level what this poem is all about, as its last stanza exclaims.

There remains one point to settle about the poem. Is the spirit of the poem submissive and fearful or is it assertive and joyous? This is one way of asking about the quality of faith in the poem. I think the answer to this question is the nature of Christianity. The Christian vision has a Good Friday which involves submission and fear. It has an Easter Sunday, individual and joyous. There is no dichotomy, only a paradox which is throughout all the gospels. This poem is an eminently Christian poem. Its spirit and tone is Ignatian. Its movement from pain to joy with Christ as the exemplar is at the very heart of

Christian doctrine, and central in the Exercises. Those who see
only the gloom have overlooked the glory:

> In a flash at a trumpet crash
> I am all at once what Christ is, since he was what I am,
>   and
> This Jack, joke, poor potsherd, patch, matchwood,
>   immortal diamond,
>   Is immortal diamond.[32]

CHAPTER FOUR

The Ignatian Spirit of the Priest-Poet

"Homo creatus est laudare."

Some preliminary remarks are necessary before examining
Hopkins' mature poetry for its Ignatian qualities. It is valuable
to recall the relationship between the Spiritual Exercises and
traditional Christian doctrine. Ignatius' conversion revolved
around the reading of three books: *The Life of Christ* (by
Ludolph of Saxony), in a Spanish translation by F. A. Monte-
sino, *The Golden Legend* (by Jacopo de Voragine, in a
Spanish translation done by Gauberto Maria Vagad), and *The
Imitation of Christ* (Spanish translation). Historians and biog-
raphers of Ignatius note that he expressed special favor for
The Life of Christ and the stories of St. Augustine, St. Francis,
St. Dominic, and St. Onuphrius, that he found in *The Golden
Legend.* These books put him in direct contact with the whole
Christian tradition. Thus it is not surprising to find that the
matter of the Exercises is made up primarily of the Bible, the
greater use being made of the New Testament. Ignatius through
Augustine reveals in his Exercises a deep awareness of sacred
history and man's part in it.

The Exercises, then, are in no way a departure from traditional Christian theology. They were composed within the very
context of orthodox Christian belief. In fact, Ignatius was very
concerned that all he had done and experienced be fully
compatible with the dogmas of the Church. He drew up for
his company a set of "Rules For Thinking With The Church,"
which are a series of prescriptions for what he considered the
proper disposition towards the Church: ". . . for our Holy
Mother the Church is guided and ruled by the same Spirit and

73

Lord that gave the Ten Commandments." He wrote in his later years, "Every internal experience that comes directly from God must be in humble harmony with the prescriptions of the Church and with obedience." It is significant that he associated "thinking with the Church" with obedience, for it suggests that such an attitude was to him consonant with the discreet discipline of the Jesuit. It is important to understand hereafter, that the passages of poetry cited as Ignatian will also be traditionally Christian and Catholic.

What is meant, then, by Ignatian? What is that particular point of view, the specific emphasis that I have designated as the Ignatian vision? Ignatius stressed a triune God of action in the Exercises: God, the Father (in the Principle and Foundation, and the First Week) Who created, punished, and disinherited man; Christ, the Son (Second, Third, and Fourth Weeks) Who became man and redeemed mankind, Who continues to send His aid to man, and asks other men to help Him in His labors; the Holy Spirit (Contemplation for obtaining Love) Who infuses into men knowledge and love of the Divine Being. Another notable aspect of the Exercises is that Christ is the central figure. For Ignatius, Christ is the supreme event in mankind's history, for through Him man's destiny is again made divine. These characteristics make up what I have called the Ignatian vision: Ignatius' world view. They represent his particular view of Christianity.

What, then, is Ignatian spirituality? It is living in accordance with the Ignatian world view. The Ignatian man has a profound awareness of the grandeur of God's works and ways. He is so taken by God's greatness, that he dedicates himself entirely to God and tries to his utmost to live his life according to God's will. There are two qualities of this spirituality which I believe are peculiarly Ignatian. The first is that the Ignatian man is a sensuous man. Unlike other Christian disciples, he does not withdraw from the world, but rather plunges into it. He is overwhelmed by the beauty of things, not only because they are beautiful in themselves, but also because they are manifestations of God. His is a sacramental view of the world. The second quality is that the Ignatian man uses all things in so far as they lead him back to God. He does not use anything that leads him away from God. Because of his sacramental view, he sees all creation as a sign of, a message from, a beckoning to, the Divine. His desire is to live fully among the things God created, live among them for the greater glory or God. He is a man dedicated, but discreetly.

What is the Ignatian man? The answer to this question lies within Ignatius' own manhood. Ignatius was a soldier in one of the noblest modes of military tradition: chivalric knighthood. His manliness rested on such noble values as absolute discipline in all matters of conduct, chivalrous decorum in all human relationships, complete fidelity and generous service to the *Reyes Católicos*. When these values were elevated and amplified above their natural plane so that they could be typified as "to distinguish oneself more" in loyalty, not to the ideals of an earthly king, but to an Eternal King, then emerged the Ignatian man, the knight of Christ, who travels the whole world serving the interests of the Lord's Kingdom in order to defeat Satan; and in the battle, to enforce stern but discreet disciplines upon himself in the manner of his King Who was crucified in order that His Standard prevail; he is always and everywhere moved by the passion to distinguish himself by maximum service rendered on those occasions and in those circumstances posing the greatest and most dangerous challenges. These are the sources of the Spiritual Exercises which find themselves expressed in such meditations as the Kingdom of Christ and The Two Standards which lead to the "Election" of Christian knighthood whose service is fully accomplished by a love that is prudent, discreet, and sanctified (Contemplation for Obtaining Love).

Now it is the burden of this study to show that Hopkins, the poet, was so deeply influenced by the ideals of Ignatius, that one cannot fully read him without taking the Spiritual Exercises into account, without understanding Ignatian spirituality. From here on throughout this reading, I shall be saying (by means of arranging the poems in a kind of Ignatian order, and by highlighting them in this order) that Hopkins' vision was Ignatian, and that he possessed in full the Ignatian spirit.[1]

More specifically, I wish to point out that those unique qualities of the spirit of Ignatius, which I have distinguished above, are especially evident in his poetry.

Also, before beginning this reading, perhaps a few general remarks about Hopkins and the Ignatian spirit would sharpen the whole analysis. I think that no one would deny that Hopkins had a very acute sensibility, and that as a poet he is one of the most sensuous. His total body poetic is a testimony of this judgment. Certainly, he possessed in large measure what estheticians call artistic sensibility. However, one cannot stop here. One must ask what individuated Hopkins' artistic nature. For one thing, it was much more perceptive than what often passes under the name of artistic sensibility. More important, however, is that in his sensitive soul there is always a motion beyond the material to the spiritual. He perceived God behind it all. It may be countered that many poets possessed this sort of transcendence, and this is quite true. But has any poet sacramentalized the world of being as he did? He was always exclaiming beauty in all things. It is not too much to say that his relation to the beauty of being was ecstatic, as highly pitched as any of the Romantic poets. Indeed, so taken was he that he distrusted his relationship to that beauty. But there is always present in his sensibility the supremacy of the beauty of the spiritual over material reality, as beautiful as the material one is. So basic was this in his sensitive soul that he talked of mortal beauty and immortal beauty. This is the very core of the matter. For Hopkins, the mortal beauty of the transient world of natural being serves to proclaim the immortal beauty of the intransient world of supernatural being. This complete sacramentalization in Hopkins' sensuousness is in the spirit of Ignatius. His was an Ignatian sensibility. I hope to make this more evident in my analysis of his mature poetry.

It is also well worth it to contrast Hopkins' insight into the transcendent God in nature with other nineteenth century poets who were struggling to insist, amid increasing scientific exposures of the inner operative secrets of nature, that nature was really somehow mysterious, sacred, and sublime, and somehow inevitably turning to a "god" in or of nature, who, if they got Him in, could not get Him above it. Wordsworth and Emerson are excellent examples of pantheistic views which locked God in nature and left Him there, perhaps because locked there He could serve as the ultimate dimension of nature without making Him the ultimate but transcendent end of man.

What, then, is man's relationship to mortal beauty? In Hopkins' own words, "To what serves Mortal Beauty?" Ignatius said that man ought to use mortal beauty in so far as it leads him back to God (a unique quality of the Ignatian spirit): all for the glory of God. Hopkins answered it many times. His answer is a perfect reflection of the Ignatian spirit. When one enjoys beauty, one is enjoying a sacrament. A sacrament involves an act of sacrifice: "Give beauty back . . . back to God, beauty's self and beauty's giver."

This Ignatian attitude is fundamental to Hopkins, for it marks the coming together of the poet and priest. It can be seen throughout most of his poetry. Indeed, it amounts to a poetic method. In poem after poem, Hopkins begins with a highly sensuous description of natural being; then there is a marked turn onto a higher plane in which the supernatural is discerned in and through the natural. There is a leap from mortal to immortal beauty. This whole poetic movement is perfectly consonant with his poetic sensibility. And he does it so often that it amounts to the major movement in his poetry. I believe that this movement is so much a result of the Ignatian influence, that it is legitimate to term it the Ignatian manner in Hopkins' poetic technique. Moreover, because this sort of poetic management is so highly compatible to the sonnet structure, I firmly believe that this is one of the important reasons that Hopkins turned to the sonnet as one of his major poetic forms.

I have remarked above that Hopkins detected a lure in mortal beauty that could prove to be insidious for him. This was not because of any evil in the beauty of natural things, *per se,* but because of man's shortsightedness, he was liable to succumb to the notion of created things as an end in themselves (rather than a means to a higher end). From the beginning, it is clear that Hopkins was very conscious of this dangerous element in his relation with the beauty of this world. He was so taken with the beauty of natural things that, perhaps, the danger was greater for him than for other men. In any event, he always felt the need for inhibiting his relationship with the natural world. As we shall see shortly, in his very earliest poetry, there is an expression of this danger which results in a melancholic quality. Again and again, a kind of asceticism undercuts his delight in natural beauty. More and more he saw death in the senses. He seems to have been searching for a relation with such beauty which satisfied both his artistic and his religious sensibility. Perhaps, this is why he did not become a painter, as was his first inclination, for it would not satisfy his religious nature, or maybe he thought it would unduly strain this nature. When he became a Jesuit priest, he was given principles on which to establish a satisfactory relation between mortal and immortal beauty. But this was not a static thing. It was a vital, dynamic relation. It had to be, since from it came his most significant poetry. There is no question that Hopkins' own humanity often upset the equilibrium of the Ignatian principles, so that at times mortal beauty seemed to be in strident conflict with immortal beauty, the poet at odds with the priest, the artistic sensibility somehow pulling against the religious. The significant fact of the matter is that the Ignatian relationship never really became unstuck from him, and, indeed, prevailed to a degree, that Jesuits, looking back and being aware of the tremendous creative urge and artistic power the man possessed, proclaim his dedication to the spirit of Ignatius. Hopkins, the artist, managed to an astonishing degree to be simultaneously both poet and Jesuit priest. I believe it was because the spirit of Ignatius provided the vision and the spirit which allowed him to fulfill both his religious and artistic natures to the degree he wished.[2]

Finally, I should like to suggest that of all those aspects of Hopkins one might examine, and the list is a long and imposing one (esthetics, psychology, poetic theory and practice, theology and personality), the central and unifying notion is the human apprehension of the divine subsidy upholding and continuing created nature. From those early glimpses into natural beauty, the shaping of Hopkins' thought could be described in its successive stages as discovering beauty, storing beauty, renewing beauty, and redeeming beauty. I use the word *beauty* designedly because I do believe that wherever Hopkins' mind and thoughts ranged, his grasp and perspective were basically artistic. The essential Hopkins is the fullness of these speculations framed as a theory to be applied and practised. This is true whether we are considering his living up to the ideals of the Society of Jesus or his practices as a poet and artist. This may seem strange when applied to a man who sometimes considered himself unable to fruitfully act; however, the truly impressive though underlying note about Hopkins' life and thought, is the strain for realization and execution. This energy is apparent in the very growth and development of his mind and art. Whatever he gathered he sought to fuse and relate in one grand theory which would be a basis of action in life and imitation in art. This strain for a total theory realized in life and art is indigenous. Whatever the source and inspiration, be it Ruskin, the Pre-Raphaelites, Plato, Aristotle, Aquinas, Suarez, Scotus, Welsh poetry, the final configuration looked toward a world view to be translated into living and creating.

Hopkins saw eternal significance in human action of which all of his speculations—philosophical, theological, and esthetic —are illuminations. His most beautiful poetry expresses dramatically that single, most sublime human act, man's invocative soul-leap through nature to the divine beyond, and this action he embellished with the best of his art. It is this "inseeing" imagination spiritualized and expressed with dramatic freshness through his penetration into the deeper springs of language and its dynamics, that most distinguishes his vision and art. This artistic stamp is specifically Ignatian, I submit, because the essence of Ignatian spirituality is a regimen and movement by grace through nature to divinity. The Ignatian universe is created, sustained, and redeemed by a Triune God who acts. The Ignatian man is correspondingly dynamic, for he discovers in nature his (and its) creativity, subsidy, and redemption through the divine agency by means of his own actions of mind and will. It is this ultimate spiritual power and significance

Ignatius envisioned in the actions of men in quest of their divine destiny, that Hopkins saw and seized for artistic imitation.

With the foregoing remarks in our minds, we can now begin a more detailed study of the Ignatian influence on Hopkins' poetry.

After one has become familiar with the Exercises, it is apparent that they profoundly informed Hopkins' poetic sensibility. Even before Hopkins became a Catholic and Jesuit, the early poems indicate that this man had a religious sensibility. In a poem which he composed sometime before 1866 he wrote:

> I have desired to go
>   Where springs not fail,
> To fields where flies no sharp and sided hail
> And a few lilies blow.
>
> And I have asked to be
>   Where no storms come,
> Where the green swell is in the havens dumb,
> And out of the swing of the sea.[3]

In another poem called, "Nondum," dated Lent, 1866, Hopkins expressed poetically his quest for the truth. The motto prefixed to the poem is, "Verily Thou Art a God that Hidest Thyself." It opens:

> God, though to Thee our psalm we raise
> No answering voice comes from the skies;
> To Thee the trembling sinner prays
> But no forgiving voice replies;
> Our prayer seems lost in desert ways . . .[4]

There is no doubt that Gerard Hopkins entered the Society of Jesus with a full and generous heart, as the Fifth Annotation of the Exercises requires, "It will much benefit him who is receiving the Exercises to enter upon them with a large heart and with liberality towards his Creator and Lord, offering all his desires and liberty to Him, in order that His Divine Majesty may make use of his person and of all he possesses according to His most holy will."[5] In a poem dated Jan. 18, 19, 1866,

Hopkins expressed beautifully the renunciation of a pure spirit being drawn to the religious life. Here is indicated his prepossession with spiritual thoughts; here is, in embryo, the highly subjective emotion and eccentricity of expression which is to mark his later and more mature work. In every stanza there is the cry of a grand renunciation—the taking of the three vows of poverty, chastity, and obedience. This poem, it seems to me, shows how predisposed Hopkins was for the reception of Ignatius' Exercises. The poem is "The Habit of Perfection," which presents the essential paradox of religion: enrichment through abnegation. All means of communication with the external world is shut off in order that the inner self be enlightened:

> ELECTED SILENCE, sing to me
> And beat upon my whorlèd ear,
> Pipe me to pastures still and be
> The music that I care to hear.
>
> Shape nothing, lips; be lovely-dumb:
> It is the shut, the curfew sent
> From there where all surrenders come
> Which only makes you eloquent.
>
> Be shellèd, eyes, with double dark
> And find the uncreated light:
> This ruck and reel which you remark
> Coils, keeps, and teases simple sight.
>
> Palate, the hutch of tasty lust,
> Desire not to be rinsed with wine:
> The can must be so sweet, the crust
> So fresh that come in fasts divine!
>
> Nostrils, your careless breath that spend
> Upon the stir and keep of pride,
> What relish shall the censers send
> Along the sanctuary side!
>
> O feel-of-primrose hands, O feet
> That want the yield of plushy sward,
> But you shall walk the golden street
> And you unhouse and house the Lord.

> And, Poverty, be thou the bride
> And now the marriage feast begun,
> And lily-coloured clothes provide
> Your spouse not laboured-at nor spun.[6]

Hopkins here reveals his awareness of discipline and restraint as a means to religious advancement. He focuses on introspection and self-analysis as the mode to spiritual perfection. The striking note here is that the "retreat" is general, in no way informed by directed methodical purgation and theological illumination, as it was to become for him under the direction and discipline of Ignatian spirituality.

After he had become a Catholic and a Jesuit, his poetry continued to reveal his ascetic nature with this difference: it had been canalized into the Ignatian vision. He began to sing of the Ignatian world. And it was a world in which the kind of abnegation expressed above was considerably enriched. In the First Week of the Exercises, Hopkins meditated on the Principle and Foundation, in which Ignatius put down the key facts of human existence. In sum, he asserted fulfillment of all nature in God if oblivion is to be avoided. In the poem, "The Lantern out of Doors" (St. Beuno's, 1877), Hopkins exhibits a much more subtle insight into religious experience after almost ten years of Ignatian discipline. Moreover, he shows poetically a new and fuller awareness of the metaphysical and theological implications in spiritual goals and their accomplishment:

> Men go by me whom either beauty bright
>   In mould or mind or what not else makes rare:
>   They rain against our much-thick and marsh air
> Rich beams, till death or distance buys them quiet.

> Death or distance soon consumes them:

> This is the end of man unless there is a God that cares:

> Christ minds; Christ's interest, what to avow or amend

THE IGNATIAN SPIRIT OF THE PRIEST-POET

> There, eyes them, heart wants, care haunts, foot
> follows kind,
> Their ransom, their rescue, and first, fast, last friend.[7]

God is the last end of man, Hopkins says with Ignatius; otherwise, man is left to his natural end, dust. In "The Sea and the Skylark," he contrasts nature's fulfillment of itself (sea and lark) with man's lack of fulfillment, the loss of his supernatural destiny:

> On ear and ear two noises too old to end
> Trench—right, the tide that ramps against the shore;
> With a flood or a fall, low lull-off or all roar,
> Frequenting there while moon shall wear and wend.
>
> Left hand, off land, I hear the lark ascend,
> His rash-fresh re-winded new-skeinèd score
> In crisps of curl off wild winch whirl, and pour
> And pelt music, till none's to spill nor spend.

Man is suffering from a colossal and aboriginal blight:

> How these two shame this shallow and frail town!
> How ring right out our sordid turbid time,
> Being pure! We, life's pride and cared-for crown,
>
> Have lost that cheer and charm of earth's past prime:
> Our make and making break, are breaking, down
> To man's last dust, drain fast towards man's first slime.[8]

"And the other things were created for man's sake, and in order to aid him in the prosecution of the end for which he was created," wrote Ignatius. Hopkins gazed at the other things and realized that God

> . . . hews mountain and continent,
> Earth, all, out; who with trickling increment,
> Veins violets and tall trees makes more and more;[9]

God is the one

> . . . that present and past,
> Heaven and earth are word of, worded by. . . .[10]

And he asks,

> And what is Earth's eye, tongue, or heart else, where
> Else, but in dear and dogged man?[11]

Man, the prime voice of creation, is to praise God for being and for all being. Each man in his own unique way is to discharge his duty to the Creator who is his destiny. The following sonnet is a minor doxology in poetic form:

> Glory be to God for dappled things—
>   For skies of couple-colour as a brinded cow;
>   For rose-moles all in stipple upon trout that swim;
> Fresh-firecoal chestnut-falls; finches' wings;
>   Landscape plotted and pieced—fold, fallow, and plough;
>   And all trades, their gear and tackle and trim.
>
> All things counter, original, spare, strange;
>   Whatever is fickle, freckled (who knows how?)
>   With swift, slow; sweet, sour; adazzle, dim;
> He fathers-forth whose beauty is past change:
>   Praise him.[12]

From its purpose of creation, Ignatius logically concluded that man ought to use creatures only in so far as they helped him attain his supernatural end. And Hopkins, who was so impressed with the beauty of God's creatures, asked:

> How to kéep—is there ány any, is there none such, nowhere
>   known some, bow or brooch or braid or brace, láce, latch
>   or catch or key to keep
> Back beauty, keep it, beauty, beauty, beauty, . . . from vanish-
>   ing away?

He knew that

The flower of beauty, fleece of beauty, too too apt to, ah! to
    fleet,
Never fleets móre . . . .

Was there any way to make beauty (spiritual perfection, "beauty-
in-the-ghost") last? With Ignatius, he answered that man keeps
true beauty by seeking Immortal Beauty through mortal beauty.
Here is Ignatius' prudent use of the things of the world:

> Resign them, sign them, seal them, send them, motion
>   them with breath,
> And with sighs soaring, soaring sighs deliver
> Them; beauty-in-the-ghost, deliver it, early now, long
>   before death
> Give beauty back, beauty, beauty, beauty, back to God,
>   beauty's self and beauty's giver.[13]

Hopkins acknowledged Ignatius' warning that when man
turned to creatures as ends in themselves, he was turning away
from God, was committing sin. He contritely confesses in an
untitled poem:

> Once I turned from thee and hid,
> Bound on what thou hadst forbid;
> Sow the wind I would; I sinned:
> I repent of what I did.[14]

He trusts that God will forgive him his sin, for He is all-merciful.
And Hopkins knows that such forgiveness will require the pay-
ment of a debt:

> I have life before me still
> And thy purpose to fulfill;
> Yea a debt to pay thee yet:
> Help me, sir, and so I will.[15]

God must remake what His creatures destroy:

> God, lover of souls, swaying considerate scales,
> Complete thy creature dear O where it fails,
>   Being mighty a master, being a father and fond.[16]

We have seen thus far Hopkins wrote poetry which expressed a world view fully consonant with the vision Ignatius wrote as the theological fundament of his Exercises. God, the Father created all, sustains all being. The rarest of His creatures is man who was disobedient, punished, and disinherited. Dependent man must now earn back his supernatural inheritance by prudent use of all lesser creatures. This is not easy because of the radical imperfection of his own nature conjoined with its counterpart in physical nature. Indeed, man and his world are irrevocably "tumbling to decay," except that Christ, the Son, is men's ". . . ransom, their rescue, and first, fast, last friend." Just as Ignatius resorted to sacred history for his world view, so does Hopkins, and just as Ignatius needs Christ to make his world view theologically meaningful, so does Hopkins. For both Ignatius and Hopkins, Christ is mankind's supreme event. We are now ready for Ignatius' rumination on the world's evil as reflected in Hopkins' poetry.

In the First Exercise of the First Week, Hopkins often meditated on what Ignatius called the First, Second, and Third Sin. In the Prelude to this Exercise, Ignatius directs the exercitant to imagine the place of the meditative matter, to make the meditation more vivid by "seeing the spot."[17] He tells the exercitant that when meditation is on invisible things, "the composition will be to see with the eyes of the imagination and to consider that my soul is imprisoned in this corruptible body, and my whole self in this vale of misery, as it were among brute beasts . . . ." This is the theme of the octave of the sonnet, "The Caged Skylark":

> As a dare-gale skylark scanted in a dull cage
>   Man's mounting spirit in his bone-house, mean house,
>   dwells—
>   That bird beyond the remembering his free fells;
> This in drudgery, day-labouring-out life's age.

> Though aloft on turf or perch or poor low stage,
>   Both sing sometimes the sweetest, sweetest spells,
>   Yet both droop deadly sometimes in their cells
> Or wring their barriers in bursts of fear or rage.[18]

The First Sin was the sin of the Angels who "coming to pride, were changed from grace into malice, and hurled from Heaven to Hell," as Ignatius described the First Sin in his Exercises. Hopkins artistically visualizes this terrible scene:

> The shepherd's brow, fronting forked lightning, owns
> The horror and the havoc and the glory
> Of it. Angels fall, they are towers, from heaven—a story
> Of just, majestical, and giant groans.[19]

The Second Sin was the sin of Adam and Eve, who through their woeful disobedience brought much corruption on the human race, as Ignatius noted, "so many men being put on the way to Hell." In the untitled poem just quoted, Hopkins depicts fallen man and his mate, the heirs of this tragedy:

> But man—we, scaffold of score brittle bones;
> Who breathe, from groundlong babyhood to hoary
> Age gasp; whose breath is our *memento mori*—
> What bass is *our* viol for tragic tones?
> He! Hand to mouth he lives, and voids with shame;
> And, blazoned in however bold the name,
> Man Jack the man is, just; his mate a hussy.
> And I that die these deaths, that feed this flame,
> That . . . in smooth spoons spy life's masque mirrored:
>   tame
> My tempests there, my fire and fever fussy.

This is indeed a hard vision, and this is the only poem in which he viewed man in such cold objectivity. He always sensed the tragic in man's predicament, and most often he pointed it out with poignant tenderness; for example, in the lines addressed to a young child, one of Eve's daughters. He called it "Spring and Fall":

MÁRGARÉT, are you gríeving
Over Goldengrove unleaving?
Leáves, líke the things of man, you
With your fresh thoughts care for, can you?
Áh! ás the heart grows older
It will come to such sights colder
By and by, nor spare a sigh
Though worlds of wanwood leafmeal lie;
And yet you wíll weep and know why.
Now no matter, child, the name:
Sórrow's spríngs áre the same.
Nor mouth had, no nor mind, expressed
What héart héard of, ghóst guéssed:
It ís the blight man was born for,
It is Margaret you mourn for.[20]

Hopkins tells us that all of man's delight in nature, in creatures, is just a light of aftertaste of that first fresh sweetness of the Garden of Eden. And this is part of what Adam and Eve caused to spoil. He says in "Spring" that "Nothing is so beautiful as spring—/ When weeds, in wheels, shoot long and lovely and lush." And he questions:

What is all this juice and all this joy?
    A strain of the earth's sweet being in the beginning
In Eden Garden.[21]

Man has lost Paradise and Death awaits him:

                    Million-fuelèd, nature's bonfire burns on.
But quench her bonniest, dearest to her, her clearest-selved
    spark
Man, how fast his firedint, his mark on mind, is gone!
Both are in an unfathomable, all is in an enormous dark
Drowned. O pity and indignation! Manshape, that shone
Sheer off, disseveral, a star, death blots black out; nor mark
                    Is any of him at all so stark
But vastness blurs and time beats level.[22]

THE IGNATIAN SPIRIT OF THE PRIEST-POET 89

One recalls the passage in "The Wreck of the Deutschland" in which the poet described some of the forms of death:

> 'Some find me a sword; some
> The flange and the rail; flame,
> Fang, or flood' goes Death on Drum,
> And storms bugle his fame.
> But wé dream we are rooted in earth—Dust![23]

Hopkins again sensed the tragedy of corruption into which the human race had fallen when he wrote "On the Portrait of Two Beautiful Young People." This is an unfinished poem in which Hopkins looks at a brother and sister, and exclaims, "O I admire and sorrow!" He describes their physical beauty, and exults, "Happy the father of these!" But he sighs:

> Man lives that list, that leaning in the will
> No wisdom can forecast by gauge or guess,
> The selfless self of self, most strange, most still,
> Fast furled and all foredrawn to No or Yes.
>
> Your feast of; that most in you earnest eye
> May but call your banes to more carouse.
> Worst will the best. What worm was here, we cry,
> To have havoc-pocked so, see, the hung-heavenward
>   boughs?
>
> Enough: corruption was the world's first woe.
> What need I strain my heart beyond my ken?
> O but I bear my burning witness though
> Against the wild and wanton work of men.[24]

Ignatius calls the Third Sin, "the particular sin of some one person who for one mortal sin has gone to Hell." This is stark tragedy, and Hopkins' sense of it is excellently displayed in his fragmentary play, "St. Winefred's Well." Caradoc was to have murdered Winefred in a wood because of lust, and the poet intended him to die impenitent. The scene is just after the murder:

. . . airy vengences
Are afoot; heaven-vault fast purpling portends, and what
    first lightning
Any instant falls means me. And I do not repent;
I do not and I will not repent, not repent.
The blame bear who aroused me. What I have done violent
I have like a lion done, lionlike done, . . .

In an agony Caradoc senses the negation of evil:

                                I must miss her most
    That might have spared her were it but for passion-
        sake. Yes,
    To hunger and not have, yet hope on for, to storm and
        strive and
    Be at every assault fresh foiled, worse flung, deeper
        disappointed, . . .

And then the thought comes crushingly:

    I all my being have hacked in half with her neck: one
        part,
    Reason, selfdisposal, choice of better or worse way,
    Is corpse now, cannot change; my other self, this soul,
    Life's quick, this kind, this keen self-feeling,
    With dreadful distillation of thoughts sour as blood,
    Must all day long taste murder.[25]

How are the Caradocs going to dig out their sin? It is only
in self that the will is law. With Ignatius, Hopkins tells us in
"The Candle Indoors" that the way to do it is:

    Come you indoors, come home; your fading fire
    Mend first and vital candle in close heart's vault:
    You there are master, do your own desire;
    What hinders? Are you beam-blind, yet to a fault
    In a neighbour deft-handed? Are you that liar
    And, cast by conscience out, spendsavour salt?[26]

Here the poet, with the directness of the Scriptures, points the way to spiritual perfection as seeing the mote in one's own eye. This is the age-old warning that the conscience must be examined without self-deceit, a meaning graphically stated in the poet's concrete images, "cast by conscience out" and "spend-savour salt." Hopkins has blended his own alliterative art with some of the qualities we think of as peculiarly biblical.

The Second Exercise in the First Week of the Exercises is a meditation on sins. In this Exercise the exercitant is asked to view himself in all the horror of every sin he has ever committed. He is to view himself as an ulcer and abscess from which so many evils have issued. Hopkins also expressed this foulness of imperfection in terms of physical corruption:

> I am gall, I am heartburn. God's most deep decree
> Bitter would have me taste: my taste was me;
> Bones built in me, flesh filled, blood brimmed the curse.
>   Selfyeast of spirit a dull dough sours. I see
> The lost are like this, and their scourge to be
> As I am mine, their sweating selves; but worse.[27]

In one of the most poetic passages in the Exercises, Ignatius sums up the effect that personal sin ought to have on the sinner:

> The fifth point is an exclamation of wonder, with intense affection, running through all creatures in my mind, how they have suffered me to live, and have preserved me in life; how the angels, who are the sword of the Divine Justice, have borne with me, and have guarded and prayed for me; how the saints have been interceding and praying for me; and the heavens, the sun, the moon, the stars, and the elements, the fruits of the earth, the birds, the fishes, and the animals; and the earth, how it is it has not opened to swallow me up, creating new hells that I might suffer in them for ever.[28]

Hopkins realized Ignatius' Second Exercise of the First Week, especially the third and fifth points, in which Ignatius evidently tried to move his exercitant to true sorrow for his dis-affection.

The Third Exercise is a repetition of the First and Second, and the fourth is made by repeating all three. The Fifth Exercise is a meditation on Hell in which Ignatius asks the exercitant to see, hear, smell, taste, and feel the lost souls in "those great fires." Hopkins poetically envisioned this in the poem already quoted, especially the terrible negation of "their sweating selves; but worse." The separation by the semicolon forces great emphasis on the last two words enforcing the comparative.

Ignatius ends the First Week with a colloquy to Christ in which the exercitant considers the loving pity and mercy that Christ has for him who has sinned so often and deserves neither pity nor mercy. If the Exercises are properly given, the exercitant should make a general confession of all the sins of his past life during the First Week. The colloquy which ends the First Week should be truly an interchange between penitent and Christ dwelling in him. If the Week begins in sinful loneliness, and during the Week the exercitant stands before his King in all the "shame of the recreant knight," as Ignatius described him, the Week ends in communion with Christ. Hopkins expressed the joy of such a communion in a poem called "The Bugler's First Communion." He describes the young man in his military dress preparing to receive Christ: "He knelt then in regimental red." He rejoices personally to ". . . serve God to serve to/Just such slips of soldierly Christ's royal ration." He depicts in dramatic fashion that sudden and ineffable experience of elevating grace when he placed the host on the young man's tongue:

> There! and your sweetest sendings, ah divine,
> By it, heavens, befall him! as a heart Christ's darling,
>   dauntless;
>   Tongue true, vaunt- and tauntless;
> Breathing bloom of a chastity in mansex fine.

This could be a poetic description of Ignatius' knight of Christ, the Ignatian man of "more" love, the Jesuit priest.

In the last part of the poem, Hopkins wishes "that sealing sacred ointment" be efficacious. He hopes that this boy, "An our day's God's own Galahad" be ". . . by a divine doom channelled, nor do I cry Disaster there." He desires that ". . . he not rankle and roam in backwheels though bound home?—" He prays for him, expressing poetically the kind of prayerful petition man must make and the kind of faith he must have, if he would reach a merciful but just God:

> . . . I have put my lips on pleas
> Would brandle adamantine heaven with ride and jar,
>   did
>   Prayer go disregarded:
> Forward-like, but however, and like favourable heaven
>   heard these.[29]

And we recall those ringing lines from "The Wreck of the Deutschland" which express the indwelling of grace:

> Thou art lightning and love, I found it, a winter and warm;
>   Father and fondler of heart thou has wrung:
> Hast thy dark descending and most art merciful then.[30]

In the Second Week, Ignatius sets before the exercitant's eyes Christ, the God-man, who took on flesh to show man the way of fulfilling his quest for perfection.[31] Hopkins asked of the Two Beautiful Young People, "Where lies your landmark, seamark, or soul's star?" And with Ignatius he replies for them, "There's none but truth can stead you. Christ is truth."[32] It is Christ who must be imitated, as he wrote in a fragment of verse, "Hope holds to Christ the mind's own mirror out / To take His lovely likeness more and more."[33]

In the Second Week the exercitant makes a contemplation called "The Kingdom of Christ," in which a temporal king is used in order to better reflect on "the life of the Eternal King." This entire contemplation seems to have had a great influence on Hopkins' poem, "The Soldier," especially that part in which Ignatius writes, ". . . if we consider the temporal king's sum-

mons to his subjects, how much more worthy of consideration
is it to see Christ our Lord, the Eternal King, and before Him
the whole world, all of whom and each in particular He calls,[34]
and says: 'My will is to conquer the whole world, and all
enemies, and thus to enter into the glory of My Father. Whoever, therefore, desires to come with Me must labour with Me,
in order that following Me in pain, he may likewise follow Me
in glory.' "[35]

Ignatius' idea of a loyal subject in the kingdom of Christ is
expressed by the poet using the same comparison as Ignatius
employed, namely, a soldier of an earthly king and one of a
heavenly king. He begins by asking, "Why do we all, seeing
of a soldier, bless him?" And he answers that the heart,

Since, proud, it calls the calling manly, gives a guess
That, hopes that, makesbelieve, the men must be no less;
It fancies, feigns, deems, dears the artist after his art;
And fain will find as sterling all as all is smart,
And scarlet wear the spirit of war there express.

It is the same in the army of Christ if one will give all of
himself, and whatsoever a man contribute to the cause in the
giving of his all, this Supreme Soldier will decorate him as no
earthly leader can. As he expressed it:

Mark Christ our King. He knows war, served this soldiering
    through;
He of all can handle a rope best. There he bides in bliss
Now, and seeing somewhere some man do all that man
    can do,
For love he leans forth, needs his neck must fall on, kiss,
And cry 'O Christ-done deed! So God-made-flesh does too:
Were I come o'er again' cries Christ 'it should be this.'[36]

Hopkins here praises with the same admiration as did Ignatius,
the nobility of the soldier who lives up to his calling. Moreover,
how much more noble is the soldier of Christ who fights bravely
under His standard. He indicates the elevation of such action
through grace by depicting Christ and his soldier as companions

in battle, and Christ, the veteran leader, decorating His under-
ling for service well done, " 'O Christ-done deed!' " He con-
cludes the poem with an assertion from Christ with which
Ignatius would have been in full accord: If He were to come
again, he would ". . . scarlet wear the spirit of war there
express." "Scarlet wear" and "war" suggest that He would again
in chivalric fashion, fight and die to win the war against sin
and death. He would make "the great sacrifice."

Hopkins regarded Christ as universal hero in, "The Loss of
the Eurydice," which is another poem about shipwreck, but is
so overshadowed by the longer, more poetically brilliant "The
Wreck of the Deutschland," that it gets little attention. The
Eurydice was overturned off Ventnor in a sudden squall. She
was a training ship, and only two of her crew survived (described in the poem). Again Hopkins discerns the presence of
God in the affairs of men. In the last section he takes up the
sorrows of those in mourning and notes that they are in vain
without grace. They must pray: "But to Christ lord of thunder/
Crouch;" and the prayer should be "Holiest, loveliest, bravest,/
Save my hero, O Hero savest."[37]

In the second part of the Contemplation of The Kingdom of
Christ, Ignatius asks the exercitant "to consider that all who
have the use of judgment and reason will offer their whole
selves for labour." This idea of fine service runs all through
the Exercises and it appears in Hopkins' poetry in numerous
places. He wrote entire poems on this subject, and some of them
are his most beautiful ones. One not so well known is "Morning
Midday and Evening Sacrifice," in which he beautifully expressed the idea of a willful and complete offering of oneself
to Christ:

> The dappled die-away
> Cheek and wimpled lip,
> The gold-wisp, the airy-grey
> Eye, all in fellowship—
> This, all of this beauty blooming,
> This, all this freshness fuming,
> Give God while worth consuming.[38]

Ignatius asserted that if one makes his oblation according to the Divine Will, an identification takes place so that he in all his actions is in union with Christ. He who hears Christ's call becomes another Christ because His call is to be like Him. Hopkins expressed the "Alter Christus" idea this way:

> . . . the just man justices;
> Keeps grace: that keeps all his goings graces;
> Acts in God's eye what in God's eye he is—
> Christ—for Christ plays in ten thousand places,
> Lovely in limbs, and lovely in eyes not his
> To the Father through the features of men's faces.[39]

The first contemplation on the first day of the Second Week is on the Incarnation. Ignatius has the exercitant "call to mind . . . how the Three Divine Persons beheld all the surface and circuit of the terrestrial globe, covered with men. And how seeing all men descending into Hell, They determined in Their eternity, that the Second Person should become Man to save the human race,[40] and thus, when the fullness of time had come, They sent the Angel Gabriel to our Lady,"

> who not only
> Gave God's infinity
> Dwindled to infancy
> Welcome in womb and breast,
> Birth, milk, and all the rest
> But mothers each new grace
> That does now reach our race—
>
> .   .   .   .
>
> Of her flesh he took flesh:
> He does take fresh and fresh,
> Though much the mystery how,
> Not flesh but spirit now
> And makes, O marvellous!
> New Nazareths in us,
> Where she shall yet conceive
> Him, morning, noon, and eve;

> New Bethlems, and he born
> There, evening, noon, and morn—
> Bethlem or Nazareth,
> Men here may draw like breath
> More Christ and baffle death.[41]

The Second contemplation is on the Nativity. Ignatius asks the exercitant to think about the journey to Bethlehem and everything that happened to Joseph and Mary while there, paying tribute to Caesar. Hopkins writes[42] of the Nativity:

> A mother came to mould
> Those limbs like ours which are
> What must make our daystar
> Much dearer to mankind;
> Whose glory bare would blind
> Or less would win man's mind.
> Through her we may see him
> Made sweeter, not made dim,
> And her hand leaves his light
> Sifted to suit our sight.[43]

He wrote about the Nativity in "The May Magnificat" with a typical Ignatian point of view towards created things, emphasizing the analogy of Mother Nature and Mother Mary; he notes the growth of everything in Spring:

> Their magnifying of each of its kind
> With delight calls to mind
> How she did in her stored
> Magnify the Lord.[44]

On the fourth day of the Second Week, Ignatius asks the retreatant to make a meditation of the Two Standards, a crucial meditation that logically follows the important and powerful Contemplation on the Kingdom of Christ and precedes the Election. The exercitant is to consider "how Christ calls and desires all under His banner: Lucifer on the contrary under his." In one of his most highly wrought poems, Hopkins meditates on the Two Standards, noting how difficult but how necessary it is for every man to choose the standard under which he shall serve. And in some of the most unusual verse techniques involving diction, meter, and rime, he acutely describes the strife of such a decision which each man indicates by the way he lives. The poem is "Spelt from Sibyl's Leaves," one which many critics have left alone because of its many difficulties. Here is the part that is pertinent to the meditation of the Two Standards:

Óur évening is over us; óur night whélms, whélms,
  ánd will end us.
Only the beak-leaved boughs dragonish damask the tool-
  smooth bleak light; black,
Ever so black on it. Óur tale, O óur oracle! Lét life, wáned,
  ah lét life wind
Off hér once skéined stained véined varíety upon, áll on twó
  spools; párt; pen, páck
Now her áll in twó flocks, two folds—black, white; right,
  wrong; reckon but, reck but, mind
But thése two; wáre of a wórld where bút these twó tell, each
  off the óther; of a rack
Where, selfwrung, selfstrung, sheathe- and shelterless, thóughts
  agáinst thoughts ín groans grínd.[45]

Ignatius held that man ought to go to God through His creatures. This is the way man ought to use them. In true Ignatian fashion, Hopkins, in the first part of this poem, describes the advent of evening in which he sees with the eyes of imagination a daily reminder for man of his coming night of oblivion and the decision that his life will eternally reveal.[46] Here is the first part of the poem:

Earnest, earthless, equal, attuneable, vaulty, voluminous, . .
  stupendous
Evening strains to be tíme's vást, womb-of-all, home-of-all,
  hearse-of-all night.
Her fond yellow hornlight wound to the west, her wild hollow
  hoarlight hung to the height

Waste; her earliest stars, earl-stars, stárs principal, overbend us,
Fíre-féaturing heaven. For earth her being has unbound, her
    dapple is at an end, as-
stray or aswarm, all throughther, in throngs; self ín self steepèd
    and páshed—qúite
Disremembering, dísmémbering áll now. Heart, you round
    me right
With: Óur évening is over us. . . .[47]

The Election climaxes the Second Week of the Exercises. It
is the high point of the Four Weeks. In the Prelude for making
the Election, Ignatius makes clear what the intention should
be: "In every good Election, as far as regards ourselves, the eye
of our intention ought to be single, looking only to the end
for which I was created, which is, for the praise of God our
Lord, and for the salvation of my soul." We know what Hopkins chose. We also know what the alternate was. If he ever
expressed poetically the kind of thinking that went into that
vital decision, it was in that sonnet which is justly acclaimed
as one of the great sonnets in English literature, "The Windhover." Here Hopkins "Elects" and celebrates his "Election."
    In the subtitle of the poem, which many critics for some
reason or other neglect, the poet initially makes clear what
standard he will serve: To Christ our Lord.[48] Then he considers the natural perfection of a windhover in flight which
is exquisitely described:

I CAUGHT this morning morning's minion, king-
    dom of daylight's dauphin, dapple-dawn-drawn Falcon, in
        his riding
Of the rolling level underneath him steady air, and striding
High there, how he rung upon the rein of a wimpling wing
In his ecstasy! then off, off forth on a swing,
    As a skate's heel sweeps smooth on a bow-bend: the hurl
        and gliding
Rebuffed the big wind.

He is attracted to this marvelous creature in its majestic act.

He views the perfect performance of the bird as an act, by
analogy, of chivalric knight-errantry:

> My heart in hiding
> Stirred for a bird,—the achieve of, the mastery of the thing!

He is attracted to the life of chivalry, a life of noble service
rendered to his earthly liege lord as this cavalier bird heroic-
like serves Nature's kingdom. He could buckle on "air, pride,
plume" as this creature has "buckled" to "brute beauty and
valour, and act." He could serve an earthly king nobly. But
there is a higher knight-errantry, a nobler chivalry, a sub-
limer standard under which to serve, a greater battle to be won,
an Eternal King to follow faithfully and lovingly.[49] This way
is harder, for it demands ultimate love. But if the challenges
are of great magnitude, the boons are everlasting. Here are
those who in answer to Ignatius' question, "what shall I do for
Christ?" choose the greater service in the battle with sin and
death. They declare themselves under His standard and openly
fight for His Kingdom and willingly undergo His hardships in
order that His Kingship be proclaimed. This is the Ignatian
Election in the Spiritual Exercises, and Hopkins' poetic statement of it:

> Brute beauty and valour and act, oh, air, pride, plume, here
>   Buckle! AND the fire that breaks from thee then, a billion
> Times told lovelier, more dangerous, O my chevalier!
>
> No wonder of it: shéer plód makes plough down sillion
> Shine, and blue-bleak embers, ah my dear,
>   Fall, gall themselves, and gash gold-vermillion.[50]

The keystone of the poem is "here/Buckle!" Such diction in
the octave as "minion," "kingdom," "dauphin," and "Falcon"
suggest the chivalric tradition. This same line of diction is in
the sestet in "beauty and valour and act," "air, pride, plume,"
and "O my chevalier!" But between the octave and the sestet,
the knightly chivalry has been transfigured from that of earthly
nobility to that of heavenly nobility. This is done in the trans-

lation of "Brute beauty and valour and act" into "air, pride, plume." The key term is quite properly in the poetic context, "Buckle," for at least three of its meanings apply equally well to the splendid bird of nature in the octave and the splendor of loving sacrifice in the sestet and to the line that poetically transforms the significance of the octave into the significance of the sestet ("Brute beauty . . . plume."). The first meaning that applies is "to fasten on," which throughout the whole poem suggests the traditional arming of the knight. Thus this has allusions to chivalric legend and to scripture (St. Paul, for example). The second meaning that has application is "to struggle, grapple, contend." This meaning also works throughout the whole poem: the bird's struggle with the wind analogous to the grapple of the chivalrous act, transformed into the sacrificial act of the knight of Christ. The third meaning, "to bend permanently," also is significant throughout the poem. Taken as discipline and control, we see its application to the falcon's command and mastery, analogous to the cavalier's strength of character in performance of his deeds, and to the regimen, abnegation, self-control, and obedience (which Ignatius stressed so heavily for the Company of Jesus) of the soldier of Christ. It should be noted that there is a movement in the meanings from positive to superlative, or, in Ignatian fashion, from earthly to heavenly chivalry, from natural virtue to supernatural grace, from "mastery" to the "fire . . . a billion times told lovelier. . . ."[51]

In Ignatius' memoirs (often called "autobiography"), there is a passage that illuminates this poem. On the 21st of March, 1522, Ignatius arrived at St. Benedict's Montserrat:

> Thus he wended his way to Montserrat, his mind constantly fixed on the great feats he longed to perform for the love of God in the service of his royal Master. And since his mind was entirely taken up with tales he had read in his beloved romances of love and books of a similar nature, he resolved to keep a vigil of arms for a whole night before the altar of Our Lady of Montserrat and to doff his usual princely garments and put on the livery of Christ.[52]

Father Paul Dudon, in his definitive book on St. Ignatius, notes that in keeping this vigil, Ignatius, by the grace of God, was uplifted to a new knighthood. Commenting on the vigil, he writes:

> How appropriately, then, he stood there in the obscurity of this sanctuary, at the feet of our Lady, in the garb of a poor man, an unknown traveler on the earth, where he no longer had any fixed place of abode. The arms which had ministered until now to his vanity, by means of which he hoped to win a name for himself, he left to Fray Juan Chanones, to be hung as an *ex-voto* in the chapel of our Lady after his departure from Montserrat. Henceforth he wished no other buckler than that of faith, no other helmet than that of salvation, no other sword than the sword of the spirit of God. And in the fervor of his prayer, he begged Mary's aid in putting on the armor of the Christian, which is Christ.[53]

The supernatural character of the armor of this knight is expressed in the last three lines of the sestet. Hopkins, as he so often does, points to nature for his illustration of the Christian knight. The turning over of the earth by a plough is his figure, and by means of skillfully selected verbs (fall, gall, gash) describing the action of the earth on the blade of the plough, he suggests the ultimate chivalry of such a knight in imitation of his King.[54] Hopkins here gives a brilliant image which with great poetic effect figuratively evaluates sacrifice for the love of God. The Election in the Spiritual Exercises is an embodiment of Ignatius' own conversion to Christ by which means he passed it on to his Company. Hopkins poetically celebrated the vital nexus between himself, and Ignatius, an oath of allegiance "To Christ our Lord."

Finally, in reading this poem, it is important to distinguish between a dedication and address. Many religious interpretations mistake Hopkins' belated dedication "To Christ our Lord" as the announcement of the subject matter of the poem, in most instances identifying the bird as symbolic of Christ Incarnate and Crucified. Now it is true that Hopkins, accepting Scotus' notion of Christ as possessing perfectly the totality of all created nature, sees mirrored in nature a gleam of this ideal perfection, but, while this undoubtedly is the ideational substructure of this sonnet as well as most of Hopkins' poetry, this poem expresses a spiritualized vision of nature by which the seer discovers in natural perfection a spiritual ideal which leads to spiritual perfection. This kind of sight is integral to Ignatius' method of meditation which he called seeing "with the eyes of imagination"; it too is intended to lead to spiritual truth and perfection. Thus I am arguing there is no symbol of Christ in the poem, no direct reference or allusion to his passion, but rather an oblique analogy which is the substratum of most Christian writing, especially Hopkins'. The ending of the sonnet, where most of the rumbles against this view would center, are images of human suffering, not of Christ crucified or triumphant. The poem is much more a statement of the value of sacrifice enhanced by what Hopkins' called "corrective" grace, the grace of renunciation. Hopkins is here expressing the stress of grace through nature which, being instressed, fills the heart with love and moves the heart to acts of love, sacrifice. Read this way, the poet's dedication makes sense.

A theme similar to Election appears a number of times in the poetry of Hopkins. It appeared in his early poetry, for example in "Myself unholy," dated June 24, 1865. In the last stanzas, Hopkins looks to Christ:

> This fault in one I found, that in another:
>
> And so, though each have one while I have all,
> No *better* serves me now, save *best;* no other
> Save Christ: to Christ I look, on Christ I call.[55]

Twenty years later, he was still singing a song of Election, though now with all of the artistry of his mature poetry. In 1885, he wrote a sonnet called, "To what serves Mortal Beauty?" This poem might be described as a meditation on mortal beauty in nature in which Hopkins considers how art tries to capture beauty to slow its fleeting pace, and answers the question with which he began the poem by stating that all natural beauty serves "God's better beauty, grace" if man will spiritualize it:

To what serves mortal beauty—dangerous; does set danc-
ing blood—the O-seal-that-so feature, flung, prouder form
Than Purcell tune lets tread to? See: it does this: keeps warm
Men's wits to the things that are; what good means—where
    a glance
Master more may than gaze, gaze out of countenance.

If man is to avoid misusing "dangerous" mortal beauty, he should "wish all, God's better beauty, grace":

Our law says: Love what are love's worthiest, were all
    known;
World's loveliest—men's selves. Self flashes off frame and
    face.
What do then? how meet beauty? Merely meet it; own,
Home at heart, heaven's sweet gift; then leave, let that alone.
Yea, wish that though, wish all, God's better beauty, grace.[56]

Again Hopkins is expressing a key Ignatian idea: mortal beauty can be repossessed on the level of the supernatural if man will use it to fulfill the purpose for which God created him. This right use is the price of repossession. W. H. Gardner, the noted Hopkins scholar, makes an important comment about this poem regarding what he calls its "clear-eyed compromise." While discussing the poem, he remarks: "Without conscious polemic, the poem is directed equally against extreme aestheti-cism and extreme puritanism. Without force or protest, the sensualist and the ascetic in Hopkins are intellectually recon-ciled. As it is foolish to reject natural blessings, so it is sinful to become 'attached' to them, for such indulgence will cloud and stupefy the finest intelligence. No, not the *finest;* for the climax of the poem implies that the highest intelligence is in-separable from the soundest moral judgment. . . . 'Then let beauty alone. Not altogether, as I have said. Beauty is justly desirable, but it is only a part of the total Good. Wish for the all-embracing higher beauty, God's grace; for that brings an insight which will show you how mortal beauty, undiminished in its essence, falls into its proper place in the scheme of things.' "⁵⁷

Another poem in which he attempts to say poetically what he believed as a Christian and Jesuit about the submission of self to God is a sonnet entitled, "St. Alphonsus Rodriguez." Alphonsus was a lay brother of the Society who acted as hall porter to the College of Palma in Majorca. He served in this capacity for thirty-seven years. His outstanding virtue was obedi- ence, in some instances so literal, that in the process of can- onization it had to be defended as an extraordinary grace of God. Alphonsus himself wrote a number of treatises on the spiritual life, one of them being a commentary on Ignatius' famous *Letter on Obedience*. Obedience to command of the superior who, as is so often expressed in the *Letter* and in the Constitutions of the Society, acts "in the place of Christ our Lord," is the most fundamental law of the Society of Jesus. There are nine rules in the Summary of the Constitutions that deal directly with obedience. As Christ did His Father's will, Ignatius intended to do Christ's will. Ignatius conceived this obedience as a soldier's discipline in following the commands of the captain. It should be immediate, unquestioning, dedi- cated conformity to the orders of appointed superiors who act "in the place of Christ our Lord." These military commands may ask for the most dangerous exploits demanding ultimate sacrifices:

> HONOUR is flashed off exploit, so we say;
> And those strokes once that gashed flesh or galled shield
> Should tongue that time now, trumpet now that field,
> And, on the fighter, forge his glorious day.
> On Christ they do and on the martyr may;

Or they may be orders for a silent secret battle within:

> But be the war within, the brand we wield
> Unseen, the heroic breast not outward-steeled,
> Earth hears no hurtle then from the fiercest fray.

Some serve God with action; some serve in patient waiting. In the inscrutable will of God Who created all and "pitched" all being, lies the solemn singular service of each of his servants. The poet (using the language of chivalry and soldiery) here tried to express the price and paradox of submission to the will of God and the glory it wins (with St. Alphonsus as his metaphor); God sustains all creation yet,

> Could crowd career with conquest while there went
> Those years and years by of world without event
> That in Majorca Alfonso watched the door.[58]

In the third week Ignatius has the exercitant meditate on the Passion and Death of Christ, so that seeing with what love Christ bore the evils of the world, he too might bear them in like manner. Hopkins indicated how deeply the Passion affected him in many places in his writing. In an early poem, for example, he expresses the profound implications of the Passion of Christ. The poem is entitled "New Readings":

> ALTHOUGH the letter said
> On thistles that men look not grapes to gather,
> I read the story rather
> How soldiers platting thorns around CHRIST'S HEAD
> Grapes grew and drops of wine were shed.[59]

In stanza 22 of "The Wreck of the Deutschland" he notes the sacredness of the numeral five:

> Five! the finding and sake
> And cipher of suffering Christ.
> Mark, the mark is of man's make
> And the word of it Sacrificed.[60]

This is but one of the stanzas in this poem given over to the Passion (all noted in the chapter on the poem), all of which are distinguished for their singular poetic intensity. This is significant since it is the first major poem that Hopkins wrote

after joining the Society of Jesus, and there is reason to believe
that the Ignatian Third Week (given to the Passion) intensely
affected him. We know this from an entry in his diary (late
1869) in which he, after the fact, objectively analyzes an emotional outburst of his:

> One day in the Long Retreat (which ended on Christ-
> mas Day) they were reading in the refectory Sister
> Emmerich's account of the Agony in the Garden and I
> suddenly began to cry and sob and could not stop.
> I put it down for this reason . . . . I remember much
> the same thing on Maundy Thursday when the pre-
> sanctified Host was carried to the sacristy. But neither
> the weight nor the stress of sorrow, that is to say of
> the thing which should cause sorrow, by themselves
> move us or bring the tears as a sharp knife does not cut
> for being pressed as long as it is pressed without any
> shaking of the hand but there is always one touch,
> something striking sideways and unlooked for, which
> in both cases undoes resistance and pierces, and this
> may be so delicate that the pathos seems to have gone
> directly to the body and cleared the understanding
> in its passage.[61]

One of the most powerful meditations on the Passion (and
implicitly the Holy Eucharist) is an early poem, "Barnfloor and
Winepress," which indicates how deeply Christ's passion affected
him as a young man. In this poem, Hopkins states the redemptive meaning of the Passion and Death of Christ:

> THOU that on sin's wages starvest,
> Behold we have the joy in harvest:
> For us was gather'd the first-fruits
> For us was lifted from the roots,
> Sheaved in cruel bands, bruised sore,
> Scourged upon the threshing-floor;
> Where the upper mill-stone roof'd His head,
> At morn we found the heavenly Bread,
> And on a thousand Altars laid,
> Christ our Sacrifice is made.

Those whose dry plot for moisture gapes,
We shout with them that tread the grapes:
For us the Vine was fenced with thorn,
Five ways the precious branches torn;
Terrible fruit was on the tree
In the acre of Gethsemane;
For us by Calvary's distress
The wine was rackèd from the press;
Now in our altar-vessels stored
Is the sweet Vintage of our Lord.

In Joseph's garden they threw by
The riv'n Vine, leafless, lifeless, dry:
On Easter morn the Tree was forth,
In forty days reach'd Heaven from earth;
Soon the whole world is overspread;
Ye weary, come into the shade.

The field where He has planted us
Shall shake her fruit as Libanus,
When He has sheaved us in His sheaf,
When He has made us bear His leaf.—
We scarcely call that banquet food,
But even our Saviour's and our blood,
We are so grafted on His wood.[62]

In the sixth point of the first contemplation, Ignatius asks the exercitant to consider how Christ suffers all the torments of the Passion for his sins, and that he ought to suffer for Christ. Thus he stated a central tenet of Christianity, that the instrument God often uses to make men over in the image of His Divine Son will be suffering, suffering for His sake. This is true imitation of Christ. This is what Hopkins is saying in the lines quoted above.

The Fourth Week of the Exercises is given over to meditation of the glorified Christ, the Resurrection and Ascension. The exercitant is told in the third prelude "to ask for grace to be intensely glad and to rejoice in such great glory and joy of Christ our Lord," and in the fifth "to regard the office of Comforter, which Christ our Lord exercises." The Resurrection is also a major theme in Hopkins' poetry. It is important in

"The Wreck of the Deutschland," as already noted;[63] he devoted at least three whole poems to it among his early poetry,
and it is the theme of one of his most beautiful sonnets among
his mature poetry.

One of the early poems is untitled. In it he tries to express
the meaning of the Resurrection. He sings a new song:

> The words are old, the purport new,
> And taught my lips to quote this word
> That I shall live, I shall not die,
> But I shall when the shocks are stored
> See the salvation of the Lord.[64]

In a poem dated Lent, 1865, he expresses the "sweetness" of
grace in "Easter Communion," that comes to those whose
"scarce-sheathed bones are weary of being bent" during the
forty days:

> Breathe Easter now; you serged fellowships,
> You vigil-keepers with low flames decreased,
>
> God shall o'er-brim the measures you have spent
> With oil of gladness.[65]

And in another early poem written about the same time,
or soon after, he hymns Easter:

> BREAK the box and shed the nard;
> Stop not now to count the cost;
> Hither bring pearl, opal, sard;
> Reck not what the poor have lost;
> Upon Christ throw all away:[66]

But it is in the sonnet of the Jesuit period, "That Nature
is a Heraclitean Fire and of the comfort of the Resurrection,"
that Hopkins in all his poetic flourish expressed Ignatius'
"glory and joy of Christ our Lord" in his triumphant Easter.
After having stated that nature has a "million-fueled" bonfire
which burns on, the poet turns to man and notes that in contrast to nature, man's mark is soon gone:

O pity and indignation! Manshape, that shone
Sheer off, disserveral, a star, death blots black out; nor mark
Is any of him at all so stark
But vastness blurs and time beats level. Enough! the Resur-
rection,
A heart's-clarion! Away grief's gasping, joyless days, de-
jection.

In the last part of the poem, as we saw in "The Windhover,"
the poet employs strongly contrasting (matchwood-diamond)
imagery which goes into brilliant poetic figuration of the triumphant meaning the Resurrection has for man:

Across my foundering deck shone
A beacon, an eternal beam. Flesh fade, and mortal trash
Fall to the residuary worm; world's wildfire, leave but ash:
In a flash, at a trumpet crash,
I am all at once what Christ is, since he was what I am, and
This Jack, joke, poor potsherd, patch, matchwood, immortal
diamond,
Is immortal diamond.[67]

The Exercises close with the Contemplation for obtaining
Love. Ignatius tells the exercitant that love of God becomes
the motive in the right use of creatures, for this is how the
soul, in Christ, through creatures goes to God. He urges the
exercitant to seek a great and abiding love for God. Hopkins
expresses the personal desire involved in such a contemplation
in the last part of his poem, "In the Valley of the Elwy," in
which he notes the solicitude of the Creator for his creature
as the only way in which man can be made perfect; seeing the
lovely "world of Wales," he makes the observation:

Only the inmate does not correspond:
God, lover of souls, swaying considerate scales,
Complete thy creature dear O where it fails,
Being mighty a master, being a father and fond.[68]

Worth noting here again is an early poem in which the poet
expresses the spirit of this Ignatian contemplation. In this

untitled poem dated October 22, 1865, he uses the image of a bird, foreshadowing the windhover image, as a symbol of his desire for God, a "changeless note" of love which has been purified from all disaffection:

> Let me be to Thee as the circling bird,
> Or bat with tender and air-crisping wings
> That shapes in half-light his departing rings,
> From both of whom a changeless note is heard.
> I have found my music in a common word, . . .[69]

In stanza 32 of "The Wreck of the Deutschland," we recall his utterance of his deep love of God: "I admire thee, master of the tides, / Of the Yore-flood, of the year's fall . . . ," and the ringing close of the same poem with a catalogue of devotional epithets expressing universal man's love for his God: ". . . Pride, rose, prince, hero of us, high-priest, / Our hearts' charity's hearth's fire, our thoughts' chivalry's throng's Lord."

In the Contemplation for obtaining Love, Ignatius has the exercitant offer himself entirely to God with great affection in what is one of his most moving prayers, which begins, "Take, O Lord, and receive all my liberty, my memory, my understanding, and all my will, whatsoever I have and possess. . . ." Hopkins caught the ecstasy of this sort of love for God in his poem, "Hurrahing in Harvest," in the last part of which he perceives in nature such beautiful epiphanies of the love of God that it almost puts him beside himself:

> I walk, I lift up heart, eyes,
>   Down all that glory in the heavens to glean our Saviour;
>   And, eyes, heart, what looks, what lips yet gave you a
> Rapturous love's greeting of realer, of rounder replies?
>   And the azurous hung hills are his world-wielding shoulder
>   Majestic—as a stallion stalwart, very-violet-sweet!—
> These things, these things were here and but the beholder
>   Wanting; which two when they once meet,
> The heart rears wings bold and bolder
>   And hurls for him, O half hurls earth for him off under
>   his feet.[70]

I have attempted to show in this section that Hopkins' poetry is truly Ignatian. I have tried to indicate through arranging poems according to the order of the Spiritual Exercises that his vision of the world was Ignatian, that time and again his poetic art originates in the Exercises, always trying to capture the authentic Ignatian spirit. Jesuits are given long and arduous training, the core of which is the Exercises which each must learn, meditate, practice, and live every day of his life. Such intense rigor profoundly affects any man who submits himself to it, and how much more the man like Hopkins who had an ascetic nature to begin with, had much in common with Ignatius before he became a Catholic and Jesuit, and who, being a convert, found the thorough-reaching depth psychology of Ignatius not only effective, but as so many of his writings indicate, absolutely overwhelming! It is no wonder then that Hopkins' acute sensibility was profoundly influenced, so that his poetic output reflected everywhere, both consciously and unconsciously, the Ignatian ideal of men crucified to the world, and to whom the world itself is crucified, all for the greater glory of God. This is what I believe Hopkins says over and over again in his poetry, and with such beauty that no Jesuit poet has matched him, let alone surpassed him. It is the major thematic pattern of his art.

Finally, no reader should interpret this section as complete approval of this centrally informing influence. Though it has been my main intent to show the high degree of harmony between the spirit of the Exercises and Hopkins' poetry, I do not mean to say that no other influence was there or counted for as much. I do mean to say with emphasis that this influence was there. Moreover, I am quite aware that since Ignatius and Hopkins were Christian, quite naturally they would share a common view. Thus that the content of the Exercises and Hopkins' poetry are Christian in matter comes as no surprise. The question is: Is Ignatian spirituality consonant with Hopkins' art? If, as I have tried to show, there is a very considerable harmony between the two, this must mean that conscious and subconscious influences came in upon the poet. This is not to say that every instance of similarity or identity denotes a debt, but rather multiple instances mark a notable and quite probable central influence.

Sometimes the criitcism is made that this cannot be because good poets just do not work this way. Since critical theory as well as the history of poetic process is so limited, I am not compelled to defend against a judgment for which there is, at best, the criteria of mere opinion.

A more important concern is whether this heavy influence was totally a good thing so far as the art is concerned. A judgment of this sort necessarily calls for a basic premise on the part of the critic, for he first has to declare himself on the importance and relevance of this vision. A Christian will tend to emphasize and approve, and the secularist to except it and be irritated by it. Apart from this separation, I think both can agree that religion is only one element in human existence and thus poetry that encompasses this element only and primarily, even significantly, has notable limitations of subject, movement, and tone. Though we are elevated and profoundly moved by such poetry, we do know there is more to life, maybe not as important to some, but more, and demand that our art reflect it. Religion itself is based on this concept and it may be the religious poet's most serious shortcoming not to take artistic cognizance of this fact. This, it seems to me, can amount to a serious limitation of scope, be the penetration ever so deep. Hopkins' poetry partakes of this limitation to an extent that might be measured by noting the number of those who, attempting critical analysis of his poetry, boldly avoid the most obvious religious implications (the "Windhover" sonnet, for example) and search diligently for alternate explications. This is not only, as some allege, anti-religion; it is in many cases the working critic's attempt to provide a wider and greater base for Hopkins' art.

Finally, Hopkins' poetry is not a poetic version of the Spiritual Exercises, but rather an artistic reflection of them as Hopkins saw their practicality in the life and actions of the spirit in quest of divinity. The active work of salvation is what

Ignatius attempted to facilitate through his Exercises, and Hopkins tried to artistically imitate men working out their salvation. The distinctive note is the dramatic quality of his art; the poise, pose, and purpose of "Manshape" whose Yes or No God Himself asks for. The dramatic action: "Grasp God, throned behind/Death. . . ."

CHAPTER FIVE

The Desolate Self of the
Terrible Sonnets

"Mine, O thou lord of life, send my roots rain."

There is a parallel between Ignatius and Hopkins which
elucidates those poems which Hopkins wrote during his last
years, and especially those that express disconsolation. Both
Ignatius and Hopkins suffered a period of intense dejection
which became crucial tests of their spirits. Both men saw their
crises as essentially religious and both tried to confront them
with dispositions and actions which might be called religious
exercises. Ignatius bequeathed to those that followed him the
fruit of his experience, which was a means to sanctity, and
Hopkins was a follower of Ignatius. Both left records of their
experiences: Ignatius wrote *The Spiritual Exercises,* Hopkins
his "terrible" sonnets.

After Ignatius left Montserrat for Barcelona, he stopped over
at the little town of Manresa. He had meant to stay there for
a few days of repose, but his stay lasted ten months, during
which time he experienced what his biographers term consolation, spiritual anguish, and mystical transformation. It was
during this time that he discovered the book which was dear
to him, the *Imitation of Christ.* The particular experiences I
wish to refer to are those months during which Ignatius suffered bitter remorse, agonizing scrupulosity, and intense spiritual disconsolation. He tells us that he was on the brink of
desperation and even suicide. He tried reading the Passion at
midnight prayer. He entered on an eight days' fast. He wrote

down all his sins. He tried giving himself over to his confessor who commanded him to stop recollecting them. All this was of no avail. Ignatius tells us that one day he threw himself on his knees and with all the fervor of soul and power of voice he could muster, he cried aloud, "Lord, help me; for I find no succor among men. Ah, if only I could find help, no price would be too dear. Do you, yourself Lord, show me the proper remedy; even though I should have to go to a little dog, I would go, if only he would lead me to the remedy." He also tells that when he was tempted to do away with himself, he gained control with the protestation, "Lord, I will do nothing to offend you."

These dark hours eventually led to the visions at Cardoner which Ignatius described as the most sublime hour of his life, for it was at this time his illumined spirit was transformed. Inigo of Loyola became Ignatius of Jesus. Later when he meditated on his experience, he was moved to write it all down in a notebook, which was to become his book of *Spiritual Exercises.*

Hopkins suffered a similar desolation during his last years, and, though I do not mean to suggest that his period of dejection had the deep spiritual implications that it had for Ignatius, I do want to point out that there are spiritual implications in Hopkins' experience, that his poetic reflections of his experiences have a striking consonance with the book that gave so much solace to Ignatius, the *Imitation of Christ,* and that these poems show forth Hopkins' attempt to discern the spirit of Christ from the spirit of darkness, which is central in Ignatian spirituality. It must not be forgotten that Hopkins' whole life was directed by the spiritual ideals of Ignatius.

Anyone who reads through the writings of Gerard Manley Hopkins will certainly be struck by what might be described as an essential sorrow that was so much a part of Hopkins' vision and which is so often the tone and theme of his poetry. Many readers know his sonnets of 1885-1889 in which the sorrow becomes the sorrow of a Lear or Hamlet, a universal sorrow that is both sublime and purgative. Despite the suggestions of some critics, it is clear that from the beginning Hopkins was essentially an idealist who could not but be downcast over the world. And this "world-sorrow" increased during his life until the last four years when it became a real desolation.

To see that there was a basic melancholy in Hopkins from the beginning, one has only to read through some of the extracts from his early diaries in which the melancholic moment appears again and again. For example, in 1864 he began a piece of prose fiction (one of two such attempts) with the following sentence: "There was neither rain nor snow, it was cold but not frosty: it had been a gloomy day with all the painful dreariness which December can wear over Clapham."[1] His diaries and notebooks are studded with poetic figures that came to him from time to time, and many of these reflect a melancholic aspect. He jotted down under April 14, 1864, "Moonlight hanging or dropping on treetops like blue cobweb."[2] Under May 3, he put down, "Snakes'-heads. Like drops of blood. Buds pointed and like the snakes' heads, but the reason of name from mottling and scaly look."[3] Under 1864 there is a two-line entry, "Tuncks is a good name. Gerard Manley Tuncks. Poor Tuncks."[4]

A perusal of the early poems of 1860-1875 makes even more obvious that there was a strong strain of melancholy in Hopkins, that this element was quite naturally a part of his ascetic nature which informs so much of his early verse. In an undated poem in the early group, entitled "Spring and Death," this sorrow is apparent:

> 'Death,' said I, 'what do you here
> At this Spring season of the year?'
> 'I mark the flowers ere the prime . . .'
> . . . .
> It seem'd so hard and dismal thing,
> Death, to mark them in the Spring.[5]

In a poem dated June 24, 1865, he shows the melancholic aspect of his ascetic nature:

Myself unholy, from myself unholy
To the sweet living of my friends I look—
Eye greeting doves bright-counter to the rook,
Fresh brooks to salt sand-teasing waters shoaly:

And they are purer, but alas! not solely
The unquestion'd readings of a blotless book.
And so my trust, confused, struck, shook
Yields to the sultry siege of melancholy.[6]

. . . .

In an early diary, 1866, there is the following entry: "For Lent. No pudding on Sundays. No tea except if to keep me awake and then without sugar. Meat only once a day. No verses in Passion Week or on Fridays. Not to sit in armchair except can work in no other way. Ash Wednesday and Good Friday bread and water."[7] It was this year that Hopkins was received into the Catholic Church. Two years later, 1868, he entered the Jesuit Novitiate at Roehampton. In 1870 he began his philosophical Studies at St. Mary's Hall at Stonyhurst. In 1874 he went to St. Beuno's College in North Wales for his theological studies.

In his journal of that year there appears the following significant passage under the date September 6:

Looking all around but most in looking far up the valley I felt an instress and charm of Wales. Indeed in coming here I began to feel a desire to do something for the conversion of Wales. I began to learn Welsh too but not with very pure intentions perhaps. However on consulting the Rector on this, the first day of the retreat, he discouraged it unless it were purely for the sake of labouring among the Welsh. Now it was not and so I saw I must give it up. At the same time my music seemed to come to an end. Yet, rather strangely, I had no sooner given up these two things (which disappointed me and took an interest away—and at the same time I was very bitterly feeling the weariness of life and shed many tears, perhaps not wholly into the breast of God but with some unmanliness in them too, sighed and panted to Him), I had no sooner given up

the Welsh than my desire seemed to be for the conversion of Wales and I had it in mind to give everything else for that; nevertheless weighing this by St.
Ignatius' rules of election I decided not to do so.[8]

This passage is significant, it seems to me, because it shows a
number of important things about Hopkins which bear heavily
on the last four years of his life when he experienced a terrible
desolation of spirit which he expressed so completely in the
sonnets of those years. First, the passage indicates his constant
intellectual vigor which continued until his death despite his
inner strife. He was always delving into something, and here
it is Welsh and music. Second, this entry shows Hopkins curb-
ing his insatiable curiosity because of a higher motive. Before he
became a Jesuit the restraint was subjective religious abnegation; after, it was guided by St. Ignatius through his Exercises.
True, the motivation is still religious, but the rule of prudent
love is Ignatian. And finally, this passage is important because
it indicates that such restraint caused weariness and enervation
especially to one with a nature that had such vibrant interests,
which was the other side of his melancholia. This sort of negation was to creep into his priestly life as well as into his artistic
endeavors until it reached its peak in the last years of his life.

Hopkins did not confide his aridness to his journals only.
His correspondence is full of references to it. After R. W. Dixon
had read his poetry, he urged him to publish: "It seems to me
that they ought to be published. Can I do anything?"[9] In
October of 1878 Dixon had asked Hopkins whether he wrote
verse. Hopkins told him about burning what he had written
before he became a Jesuit, and said that except for a few presentation pieces he wrote nothing for seven years until on the
hint of his superior he wrote a poem commemorating the wreck
of the Deutschland: ". . . I offered it to our magazine the
Month, though at first they accepted it, after a time they with-
drew and dare not print it. After writing this I held myself
free to compose, but cannot find it in my conscience to spend
time upon it; so I have done little and shall do less. . . . But
even the impulse to write is wanting, for I have no thought of

publishing."[10] Despite this statement, which was made about a year before Dixon had read some of Hopkins' verse, Dixon, hoping to facilitate publishing, offered to say something about his poetry in the volume of Church History he was then working on. Hopkins' answer was still in the negative:

> It was of course a very great pleasure to have so high an opinion expressed of my poems and by you.
> But what concerns the notice you kindly offer to make of me in your forthcoming volume, it would not at all suit me. For this there are several reasons, any one sufficient; but it is enough to say now that (1) I have no thought of publishing until all circumstances favour, which I do not know that they ever will, and it seems that one of them shd. be that the suggestion to publish shd. come from one of our own people; (2) to allow such a notice would be on my part a sort of insubordination to or doubledealing with my superiors. But nevertheless I sincerely thank you for your kind willingness to do me a service.[11]

Hopkins' failure to publish during his lifetime, though on a few occasions he half-heartedly tried, is a sort of symbol of the lifelong frustration of his creative instincts, for lacking publication of some sort, he lost eventually the drive to compose the little his conscience would permit him in his chosen state. And it must be remembered that this restraint was self-imposed, a quite scrupulous interpretation of his priestly vocation.

Six months before Dixon brought up the matter of publication, Robert Bridges queried him about it. Hopkins' answer substantiates my analysis of his failure to publish and his creative urge:

> When I say that I do not mean to publish I speak the truth. I have taken and mean to take no step to do so beyond the attempt I made to print my two wrecks in the *Month*. If some one in authority knew of my having some poems printable and suggested my doing it I shd. not refuse, I should be partly, though not alto-

gether, glad. But that is very unlikely. All therefore
that I think of doing is to keep my verses together in
one place—at present I have not even correct copies—,
that, if anyone shd. like, they might be published after
my death. And that again is unlikely, as well as remote.
I could add other considerations, as that if I meant
to publish at all it ought to be more or ought at least
to be followed up, and how can that be? I cannot in
conscience spend time on poetry, neither have I the in-
ducements and inspirations that make others compose.
Feeling, love in particular, is the great moving power
and spring of verse and the only person that I am in
love with seldom, especially now, stirs my heart sensi-
bly and when he does I cannot always "make capital"
of it, it would be sacrilege to do so.[12]

W. H. Gardner describes the years after Hopkins' ordination
to the priesthood (September, 1877) until he went to Ireland
in 1884 with considerable insight into both the professional
and personal elements involved:

As a hard-working priest he was probably somewhat
more successful than he claimed to be; but as a poten-
tial mystic and dreamer, as an artist passionately devoted (with Christian reservations) to aesthetic ideals,
and always eager (despite his conscience) to write
poetry and music, he could not maintain that degree
of concentration which is so necessary for the practical,
professional man. Suffering throughout life from a
certain nervous debility, he was dogged by a sense of
failure; he was also extremely sensitive to environment,
and was horrified and indignant when he saw the
squalor of our great industrial towns. In Liverpool
and Chesterfield, he tells us, his muse turned "sullen."[13]

In 1881 R. W. Dixon wrote to Hopkins: "But first I hope that
you are going on with poetry yourself. I can understand that
your present position, seclusion and exercises would give your
writings a rare charm—they have done so in those I have seen:
something that I cannot describe, but know to myself by the

inadequate word *terrible pathos*—something of what you call temper in poetry: a right temper which goes to the point of the terrible; the terrible crystal."[14] This provoked an explanation from Hopkins of why he had not made a concerted effort to publish his verse, why he could not devote more time to his creative instinct even though denying it brought frustration, indeed, the why of his life:

> This I say: my vocation puts before me a standard so high that a higher can be found nowhere else. The question then for me is not whether I am willing (if I may guess what is in your mind) to make a sacrifice of hopes of fame (let us suppose), but whether I am not to undergo a severe judgment from God for the lothness I have shewn in making it, for the reserves I may have in my heart made, for the backward glances I have given with my hand upon the plough, for the waste of time the very compositions you admire may have caused and their preoccupation of the mind which belonged to more sacred or more binding duties, for the disquiet and the thoughts of vainglory they have given rise to. A purpose may look smooth and perfect from without but be frayed and faltering from within. I have never wavered in my vocation, but I have not lived up to it. I destroyed the verse I had written when I entered the Society and meant to write no more; the *Deutschland* I began after a long interval at the chance suggestion of my superior, but that being done it is a question whether I did well to write anything else. However I shall, in my present mind, continue to compose, as occasion shall fairly allow, which I am afraid will be seldom and indeed for some years past has been scarcely ever, and let what I produce wait and take its chance; for a very spiritual man once told me that with things like composition the best sacrifice was not to destroy one's work but to leave it entirely to be disposed of by obedience. But I can scarcely fancy myself asking a superior to publish a volume of my verses and I own that humanly there is very little likelihood of that ever coming to pass. And to be sure if I

> chose to look at things on one side and not on the
> other I could of course regret this bitterly. But there
> is more peace and it is the holier lot to be unknown
> than to be known.[15]

Here is a detailed explanation of his motivations. He had chosen
a way of life which, *as he viewed it,* demanded all of him in
the service and love of God. He was of that class of men of
that mode of humility who, Ignatius denotes in his Exercises,
must sacrifice all, no matter how painful, for the honor and
glory of God. From the beginning this was so for Hopkins, and
Ignatius' counsels in the Exercises served, no doubt, to confirm
and direct this ascetic urge in his nature.

We need not guess about this matter. Hopkins' life was
being directed by St. Ignatius, and ultimately it is to Ignatius
that we must look for a sufficient explanation of the way that
Hopkins lived his life. Hopkins himself confirms the direction
of our search:

> When a man has given himself to God's service,
> when he has denied himself and followed Christ, he
> has fitted himself to receive and does receive from God
> a special guidance, a more particular providence. This
> guidance is conveyed partly by the action of other men,
> as his appointed superiors, and partly by direct lights
> and inspirations. If I wait for such guidance, through
> whatever channel conveyed, about anything, about my
> poetry for instance, I do more wisely in every way than
> if I try to serve my own seeming interests in the matter.
> Now if you value what I write, if I do myself, much
> more does our Lord. And if he chooses to avail him-
> self of what I leave at his disposal he can do so with a
> felicity and with a success which I could never com-
> mand. And if he does not, then two things follow; one
> that the reward I shall nevertheless receive from him
> will be all the greater; the other that then I shall know
> how much a thing contrary to his will and even to my
> own best interests I should have done if I had taken
> things into my own hands and forced on publication.
> This is my principle and this in the main has been my

practice: leading the sort of life I do here seems easy, but when one mixes with the world and meets on every side its secret solicitations, to live by faith is harder, is very hard; nevertheless by God's help I shall always do so.[16]

Hopkins' "principle" here is the Principle and Foundation of the Ignatian Exercises: "Man was created to praise, reverence, and serve God our Lord, and by this means to save his soul; and the other things on the face of the earth were created for man's sake, and in order to aid him in the prosecution of the end for which he was created. Whence it follows, that man must make use of them in so far as they help him to attain his end, and in the same ways he ought to withdraw himself from them in so far as they hinder it." His reasoning is the reasoning of Ignatius on which is based all the Spiritual Exercises. And it is significant that Hopkins picked as his example the publication of his poetry, for this is the external sign of the source of the tensions that aggravated him more and more: the poet and the priest. The priest dominated the poet but not without a "war within," making, undoubtedly, this domination for the glory of God irksome, painful, and at times seemingly unbearable. Perhaps under these tensions Hopkins wrote some of his most sublime religious verse.

He explained to R. W. Dixon the attitudes of the Society toward culture, especially literature, and his explanation is simply an exposition of Ignatius' directives regarding this matter. It is significant that what he wrote here is in the fullness of the Ignatian spirit; there is no subjective argumentation, no personal bewailing. There is settled conviction:

Our Society values, as you say, and has contributed to literature, to culture; but only as a means to an end. Its history and its experience shew that literature proper, as poetry, has seldom been found to be to that end a very serviceable means. We have had for three centuries often the flower of the youth of a country in numbers enter our body: among these how many poets, how many artists of all sorts, there must have been! But there have been very few Jesuit poets and, where they have been, I believe it would be found on examination that there was something exceptional in their circumstances or, so to say, counterbalancing in their career. For genius attracts fame and individual fame St. Ignatius looked on as the most dangerous and dazzling of all attractions.[17]

Again we are told that the reason that there have not been more Jesuit artists and more famous ones is because of the very spirit of the Society, because Ignatius believed that all of this served the purpose of self and not the end of self, God. He went on to enumerate some of the Jesuits who have become known for their artistry (Beschi, Southwell, Campion, Segers) and then comments how often artistic traits, often great ones, are hidden for the greater glory of God. "Brilliancy does not suit us," he remarks, ". . . St. Ignatius himself was certainly, every one who reads his life will allow, one of the most extraordinary men that ever lived; but after the establishment of the Order he lived in Rome so ordinary, so hidden a life, that when after his death they began to move in the process of his canonization one of the Cardinals, who had known him in his later life and in that way only, said that he had never remarked anything in him more than in any edifying priest."[18] At the end of this long passage on the Jesuits, Hopkins wrote what amounts to the essence of nis vocation as he understood the life wholly dedicated to God: "I quote these cases to prove that show and brilliancy do not suit us, that we cultivate the commonplace outwardly and wish the beauty of the king's daughter the soul to be from within."[19]

In 1884 Hopkins was appointed Professor of Classics in University College, Dublin, in which had been incorporated what was left of Newman's Catholic University. He was also *ex officio* a Fellow of the Royal University. The old melancholy stayed with him. In his first letter to Bridges from Dublin, he wrote: "I have been warmly welcomed and most kindly treated. But Dublin itself is a joyless place and I think in my heart as smoky as London is: I had fancied it quite different."[20] A year later the tensions had if anything increased considerably. On May 17, 1885, he wrote to Bridges: "I must write something, though not so much as I have to say. The long delay was due to work, worry, and languishment of body and mind —which must be and will be; and indeed to diagnose my own case . . . I think that my fits of sadness, though they do not affect my judgment, resemble madness. Change is the only relief, and that I can seldom get."[21]

It might seem to the reader of Hopkins' correspondence that I have exaggerated this melancholic strain considerably. There are many letters which display a fine sense of humor; there are others which show how vigorous was his interest in the arts, and how much he delighted in them even in the last years in Dublin. But all his life the workaday world worried him; "Time's tasking" increased until what was at first a moment became long protracted periods of moroseness and dejection, the culmination taking place in the last years at Dublin. We need not speculate at any great length on this matter. We have Hopkins' own words in a letter written to a lifelong friend, A. W. M. Baillie; after a year in Ireland, he explicitly views this melancholic disposition throughout his whole lifetime:

> I think this is from a literary point of view (not a moral) the worst letter I ever wrote to you, and it shall not run much longer. You will wonder I have been so long over it. This is part of my disease, so to call it. The melancholy I have all my life been subject to has become of late years not indeed more intense in its fits but rather more distributed, constant, and crippling. One, the lightest but a very inconvenient form of it, is daily anxiety about work to be done, which makes me break off or never finish all that lies outside that work. It is useless to write more on this: when I am at the worst, though my judgment is never affected, my state is much like madness. I see no ground for thinking I shall ever get over it or ever succeed in doing anything that is not forced on me to do of any consequence.[22]

Ireland began to seem to Hopkins a sort of exile, as it had
for so many Englishmen before him. In a letter to Bridges,
September 1, 1885, he makes a reference to some sonnets that
he had written. Some scholars and critics (Gardner and Bridges,
for example) feel this is reference to the so-called terrible
sonnets: "I shall shortly have some sonnets to send you, five or
more. Four of these came like inspirations unbidden and against
my will. And in the life I lead now, which is one of a con-
tinually jaded and harassed mind, if in any leisure I try to do
anything I make no way—nor with my work, alas! but so it
must be."[23]

In one of these sonnets, he pitifully expressed a feeling of
exile because of which he was cut off from the water of encouragement and so everything he attempts remains but a start:

> To seem the stranger lies my lot, my life
> Among strangers. Father and mother dear,
> Brothers and sisters are in Christ not near
> And he my peace my parting, sword and strife.
>   England, whose honour O all my heart woos, wife
> To my creating thought, would neither hear
> Me, were I pleading, plead nor do I: I wear-
> y of idle a being but by where wars are rife.
>
>   I am in Ireland now; now I am at a third
> Remove. Not but in all removes I can
> Kind love both give and get. Only what word
> Wisest my heart breeds dark heaven's baffling ban
> Bars or hell's spell thwarts. This to hoard unheard,
> Heard unheeded, leaves me a lonely began.[24]

A letter confirms what this poem expresses: an exile from encouragement. Hopkins wrote to Bridges on May 17, 1885:
"There is a point with me in matters of any size when I must
absolutely have encouragement as much as crops rain; After-
wards I am independent. However I am in my ordinary circumstances unable, with whatever encouragement, to go on with
Winefred or anything else. I have after long silence written two
sonnets, which I am touching: if ever anything was written in

blood one of these was."[25] Bridges suggests that this poem was "Carrion Comfort," but neither can be identified with any certainty.

As the last four years of Hopkins' life passed, more and more his correspondence began to reflect spiritual as well as physical struggle. On August 7, 1886, he wrote to R. W. Dixon: "It is not possible for me to do anything, unless a sonnet, and that rarely, in poetry with a fagged mind and a continual anxiety; but there are things at which I can, so far as time serves, work, if it were only by snatches."[26] On January 27, 1887, he wrote to Dixon: "I have done some part of a book on Pindar's metres and Greek metres in general and metre in general and almost on art in general and wider still, but that I shall ever get far on with it or, if I do, sail through all the rocks and shoals that lie before me I scarcely dare to hope and yet I do greatly desire, since the thoughts are well worth preserving . . . ."[27]

If one were to pick that passage which sums up the desolation of the last years, more than likely it would be the passage from a letter to Bridges on January 12, 1888. In this passage Hopkins bluntly expressed his great dejection and the reason for it:

> At Monasterevan I tried to get some outstanding and accumulated sonnets ready for hanging on the line, that is in my book of MS, the one you wrote most of, and so for sending to you. All however are not ready yet, but they will soon be. I could send one tonight if time served, but if possible I should like to despatch this letter. It is now years that I have had no inspiration of longer jet than makes a sonnet, except only that fortnight in Wales: it is what, far more than direct want of time, I find most against poetry and production in the life I lead. Unhappily I cannot produce anything at all, not only the luxuries like poetry, but duties almost of my position, its natural outcome—like scientific works. I am now writing a quasi-philosophical paper on the Greek Negatives: but when shall I finish it? or if finished will it pass the censors? or if it does will the *Classical Review* or any magazine take it?

All impulse fails me: I can give myself no sufficient reason for going on. Nothing comes: I am a eunuch —but it is for the kingdom of heaven's sake.[28]

G. F. Lahey warns us about overstating Hopkins' sorrow: "We may discern a triple sorrow which descended on the shoulders of Hopkins, but it did not in any degree eclipse his peace and happiness."[29] Father Lahey lists as the first sorrow the inconvenience that arose from the semi-annual examination of candidates. He comments, "Hopkins was never a man of practical affairs . . . and when the board were crying for the returns, they found poor Gerard, at three A.M., his head swathed in wet towels, harassed with scruples at the award or non-award of half-marks!" Again he warns, "But to imagine that a few weeks of distasteful work darkened his whole life is manifestly absurd."

He lists as the second sorrow the political atmosphere that existed in Ireland when Hopkins was in Dublin. The Catholic support given to the Irish cause worried him a great deal. Hopkins wrote to Cardinal Newman, "Politically, the times are most troubled. I live, I may say, in an air most painful to breathe and this comes home to me more, not less, with time."[30]

Father Lahey writes of a third sorrow from which, he believes, resulted the terrible sonnets: "It sprang from causes which have their origin in true mysticism. Hopkins, smiling and joyful with his friends, was at the same time on the bleak heights of spiritual night with his God."[31] We know that from the beginning the artist and the ascetic were in contention, and that under the psychological structure of the Spiritual Exercises the artist more often seemed to Hopkins to be so unrelated to the purposes of his vocation that, at times, the artistic desires of his nature were a violation of his conscience, contrary to his solemn vows. W. H. Gardner believes that this was one of the reasons for Hopkins' neurasthenia: "The partial frustration of Hopkins's creative instincts was no doubt one of the causes of his neurosis. . . ."[32]

We are not forced to speculate to any inordinate degree that this was the source of trouble. Before the youthful Hopkins had actually decided to take holy orders, he wrote to his friend, Baillie, about the state of his health, about the two choices he saw for himself in life, and the reason why he decided on the religious life rather than that of the dedicated artist. This early revelation of his crosscurrents was written while he was teaching at Newman's Oratory following his graduation from Oxford:

> I must say that I am very anxious to get away from this place. I have become very weak in health and do not seem to recover myself here or likely to do so. Teaching is very burdensome, especially when you have much of it: I have. I have not much time and almost no energy—for I am always tired—to do anything on my own account. . . . I am expecting to take orders and soon, but I wish it to be secret till it comes about. Besides that it is the happiest and the best way it practically is the only one. You know I once wanted to be a painter. But even if I could I wd. not I think, now, for the fact is that the higher and more attractive parts of the art put a strain upon the passions which I shd. think it unsafe to encounter. I want to write still and as a priest I very likely can do that too, not so freely as I shd. have liked, e.g. nothing or little in the verse way, but no doubt what wd. best serve the cause of my religion.[33]

It is safe, I think, to attribute a good many of the unhappy moments of Hopkins' life to his poor health and to that "partial frustration" of his esthetic nature, for these sacrifices, indeed, were the source of much of his difficulty. But he always had a solace for these denials in his life dedicated to God through his vocation to the Jesuit priesthood. All these he could suffer for the greater honor and glory of God. But in the last four years of his life, a spiritual dryness set in.[34] He no longer received the solace of his priesthood. This is the third sorrow which Lahey writes of, and of which was born the "terrible pathos" of the sonnets of those years. Most of the modern critics have gone to Freud for their explanation of these poems.

Father Lahey directs us to the writers of mysticism: St. Teresa, St. John of the Cross, Poulain, Maumigny.

No one who reads through St. John of the Cross, for example, can deny that there is a parallel between what Hopkins expresses in his sonnets and what St. John describes in the Chapter entitled, "The Dark Night."[35] In fact, St. John himself writes in images relevant to Hopkins as well as the so-called mystical poets. In this Chapter, St. John describes the action of Divine Love on the soul of man as analogous to the way that material fire acts on wood. It dries the wood and removes its sap, blackens its appearance and chars it. Then the wood begins to burn in the flames until it is entirely transformed into fire. By analogy, St. John tells us, the fire of Divine Love acts the same way on the human soul. The Divine Love purges the evil tendencies of the soul by blackening its vanity and charring its egoism until, once purified, it is united to divine Love itself. One poetic expression of this are the lines from Francis Thompson's "The Hound of Heaven": "Ah! must —/Designer infinite!—/Ah, must Thou char the wood ere Thou canst limn with it?"[36]

This suggestion by Hopkins' first biographer has been dismissed by most contemporary scholars for the wrong reason, namely, that Hopkins was not a mystic and did not write mystical poetry. I believe this to be true, but this is no reason to dismiss the suggestion. During a retreat Hopkins made at Beaumont in November, 1878, he came across a volume of the writings of Marie Lataste, a French girl (1822-47) who between the ages of fourteen and twenty was supposed to have had visions of Christ and Mary when she assisted at Mass. Upon the advice of her parish priest, she wrote down her experiences which were eventually published and enjoyed a mild popularity in Catholic circles. Hopkins copied out six lengthy extracts from her writings into his notes. Her statements about the ways that God moves the world seems to have influenced his thinking regarding grace, personality, and free will. However, what is significant is his ready acceptance[37] of Marie's experiences as revealed insights into the central Christian mysteries even though their official value has never been assessed. Add to this those

passages in his note-books wherein Hopkins remarks that he
had special lights regarding certain of his speculations or meditations, and it becomes harder to dismiss Father Lahey's suggestion.

In following this directive, I have been led to try to answer
why Hopkins suffered from a mild but persistent melancholia
most of his life, why his conscience seemed to grow ever more
tender despite the generous fulfillment of the essentials of his
vocation, why the artist in him had to be so often rejected, why
he suffered and fought such a fierce inner struggle during the
last years of his life. I have already traced the biographical thread
that strings together these last poems, but the mission to Dublin, his poor health and periodic loads of examination papers,
even his inability to finish any of his endeavors are not satisfactory explanations of these last years.

Some scholars have considered whether Hopkins' attachment
to Scotus was too great thus bringing upon him limitations by
his superiors; others have thought that he worked out a grand
scheme based on Scotus and Ignatius which, he finally realized,
did not come to any true significance. This possibly caused him
to lose heart, turn sour, give over his efforts. While all of these
may have played their parts, I am still unsatisfied with them.
I think there is something even more basic to his distress.
Thomas Merton, for example, finds his vocation no bar to
voluminous publication including poetry even though he chose
to enter one of the strictest religious orders within the Church.
Why did Hopkins less than a hundred years ago find it necessary to supress the artist in himself? Was it because he had a
mistaken notion of Ignatius' rules or that he misapplied them?

The answer lies, I suggest, in Hopkins' ascetic nature nur-
tured on a very long tradition of spiritual writings of the early
saints and other spiritual books of mystical emphasis which have
as their basic perspective a rejection of all creatures.[38] *The
Imitation of Christ,* which is prescribed reading for Jesuits, is
an excellent example of this contempt of the world. It preserves
perhaps one of the earliest emphases of Christianity, that of
withdrawal and retreat from the City of Man; moreover, it
stridently underscores an opposition between nature and grace

as an explanation and justification of suffering and sacrifice as a necessary spiritual state of one's soul, if it is to advance in spiritual perfection. This character is often noted as peculiar to the "desert Christianity" of the early Church, and called Eastern Christianity. This notion is prominent in the writings of the theologians throughout the first thousand years of Christian teaching; it is central to what is known as the Patristic tradition.

By forming his conscience as he did, Hopkins chose to ignore a major Western emphasis in the second thousand years of the Christian way of life, strangely enough, one which the founder of his Order understood so well, and which he incorporated into the very foundation of his spirituality: man should use creatures insofar as they help him attain his divine destiny, even though it meant going into the world, a distinctive mark of the Jesuit order. Ignatius counseled proper use, not outright rejection. Could not Hopkins have praised God through his poetry with a clear conscience according to Ignatian spiritual ideals? Not only could he do so, but he was bound to do so if, in prudence, it sustained and advanced his spiritual life. But did Ignatius so modify Kempis? After all, the *Imitation* had a powerful influence on Ignatius, and some of its spiritual methodology was incorporated in the Spiritual Exercises. We have seen how rigidly Hopkins interpreted his life by the Ignatian regimen, how uncompromising he was about giving any leeway to any other than specifically priestly endeavors.

Dr. Gardner makes the suggestion: "Whoever would understand Hopkins must go not to Freudian psychology but rather to the 'Spiritual Exercises' of St. Ignatius Loyola, the founder of the Society of Jesus. Loyola was a great psychologist, and the religious values for which he and his disciple Hopkins stood have never been confuted, though they have often been rejected or ignored."[39] This is an obvious place to go in order to illuminate those highly astringent poems of the last years. Possibly the answer lies in the relationship between Kempis and Ignatius, the *Imitation* and the *Spiritual Exercises*.

There is undoubtedly, for example, a most intimate relationship between the *Imitation of Christ* and the directions for distinguishing the things of God that Ignatius put into his Exercises. Ignatius himself wrote, "It was at Manresa that I saw the *Gerçonzito* for the first time, and since then there is no other book of devotion that I like more." The *Gerçonzito* is one of the many Spanish editions of the *Imitation of Christ.* Kempis' book is one of the most important devotional books in the long tradition of Christian perfection. It put Ignatius in direct contact with early traditional Christian spirituality. It is significant that he made excerpts from it with great diligence, "entering with his own hand the 'more important matters,' after going over them prayerfully, into a notebook of three hundred densely crowded quarto pages."[40] It is not surprising, after the Manresa mystical experiences, when Ignatius was composing his book of Exercises, that his reverence for the *Imitation* should be strongly reflected.[41]

Moreover, much of the matter in the Exercises dealing with the problem of spiritual desolation must have come from the *Imitation of Christ,* for Kempis gave very considerable treatment to this subject in his book. Ignatius entitled the section that he wrote in the Exercises, "Rules For The Discernment of Spirits." Here Ignatius was handing down to his companions the victorious strategy of his own spiritual battles. True to his military nature, he wrote that the enemy "acts likewise as a military chief does in order to get possession of and to despoil the object of his desires." He goes on to describe how the enemy general studies, probes, feints, explores, and "where he finds us weakest, and in greatest need as regards our eternal salvation, there he makes his attack, and strives to take us by storm."[42]

In Rule IV Ignatius defines Spiritual Desolation: "I call desolation . . . as darkness and disquiet of soul, an attraction towards low and earthly objects, the disquiet of various agitations and temptations, which move it to diffidence, without hope and without love, when the soul finds itself slothful, tepid, sad, and, as it were, separated from its Creator and Lord."[43] Kempis wrote: "It is not hard to despise all human consolation when we have divine. But it is much, and very much, to be able to forego all comfort, both human and divine, and to be willing to bear this interior banishment for God's honor, and to seek one's self in nothing, nor to think of one's own merit."[44] And again: "A man must have a great and a long conflict within himself before he can learn fully to overcome himself and to direct his whole affection towards God."[45]

Now, while both Kempis and Ignatius describe desolation as a part of Christian perfection, it is most significant that Ignatius considers this an unusual state of soul, one which he urges his followers to get out of as soon as possible, for, barring the special intervention of God Himself, such a state leads but to disloyalty. For Ignatius, the natural state of soul is consolation, for in this state the soul advances in Christian perfection because it chooses and desires the True and the Good, God Himself. This is true obedience. It leads to true charity. My reading of the *Imitation* leaves me with the distinct impression that spiritual desolation is more often the normal state of the soul seeking Christian perfection. If true charity is to be had, then there must be long conflict, internal suffering, a division between desire and choice, a complete rejection of all human consolation, an utter banishment of self. I do believe Ignatius modified Kempis. These Rules he wrote are modifications.

Father Christopher Devlin suggests that Hopkins put too much reliance on Scotus' distinction between the "elective will" and the "affective will," that at times Hopkins wrote as if there were inevitable opposition between choice and desire (which I see in Kempis, and, by the way, in John of the Cross), even though his writings make clear he understood Scotus and Ignatius who both stress consolation as the normal state. He also suggests, since this emphasis does not come either from Scotus or Ignatius, it quite possibly could have come from what is sometimes called the Victorian temper or Victorianism, namely, a presumed cleavage between duty and desire in every instance. While all of these could have had their influence, I do not see how they fully explain Hopkins' frequent contravention in his own life of what he held to be true and prudent. In constantly denying and rejecting the artist in himself[46] he was rejecting his true self, I submit, and it finally caught up with him in the last years in Dublin, during which period his death is but an anticlimax to the death of his poetic genius. He denied the poet in him all his life contrary to both his intellectual and spiritual guides, the inevitable result of this being frustration, tension, sterility, and finally desolation. He does not seem to have applied prudently Ignatius' directive regarding the "proper use of creatures."

I find this very much like a Graham Greene plot wherein a brilliant poet subverts his God-given talent to a lifetime of grading examination papers of dullard schoolboys as a manifestation of his love of God, thus causing him to live a life fraught with disappointment, waste, and unhappiness. This is, of course, a caricature of Hopkins' life. I suppose that this opposition between the poet and priest in Hopkins will remain, for the most part, a mystery, which, interestingly, favors Hopkins. Despite this lifelong inner conflict (it is apparent in his earliest writing), the artist often joined the priest in making some exquisite art; despite the final and utter rejection of this art and artistry, it has curiously survived and taken an imposing place in English letters. Among the last private notes Hopkins wrote, he consigned his compositions to the care of the Lord to be used as He saw fit. He wrote, "And this I believe is heard." It is indeed very hard to question Hopkins' judgment all along the line. And what might have been is so overwhelmingly vulnerable to what was.

II

Then what, if anything, is Ignatian about these last poems Hopkins wrote? They are interestingly Ignatian in two ways. First, they show an affinity to the *Imitation of Christ* precisely as they are expressions of the spiritual desolation, which Kempis draws out so well, that Ignatius himself experienced and which were such a solace to him; and they dramatize Hopkins' artistic reflections of his attempt to use Ignatius' Rules in order to raise himself out of his desolation into a state of spiritual consolation. Hopkins' artistic reflection of a nagging religious aridity goes back to his earliest verse. Before he became a

Catholic or a Jesuit, he expressed in an early poem something
of the desolation he was to experience in his later life:

> My heaven is brass and iron my earth:
> Yea iron is mingled with my clay,
> So harden'd is it in this dearth
> Which praying fails to do away.
> Nor tears nor tears this clay uncouth
> Could mould, if any tears there were.
> A warfare of my lips in truth,
> Battling with God, is now my prayer.[47]

There was in his religious experience a perpetual "battling
with God."[48] He wrote in his first poem as a religious, "The
Wreck of the Deutschland," of this spiritual conflict:

> I did say yes
> O at lightning and lashed rod;
> Thou heardst me truer than tongue confess
> Thy terror, O Christ, O God;
> Thou knowest the walls, altar, and hour and night:
> The swoon of a heart that the sweep and the hurl of thee
> trod
> Hard down with a horror of height:
> And the midriff astrain with leaning of, laced with fire of stress.[49]

In Rule II, Ignatius warns of the battle that may take place in
those wanting to advance their spiritual lives: "In those who
go on earnestly rooting out their sins, and advancing daily
from good to better in the service of God our Lord, . . . it belongs to the evil spirit to cause anxiety and sadness, and to
place obstacles in the way, disquieting the soul by false reasons,
so that it make no further progress."[50] He goes on to explain
the causes of the strife: "There are three principal reasons why
we find ourselves in desolation. The first is because we are tepid,
slothful, or negligent in our spiritual exercises . . . . The second
reason is that God may try how much we are worth, and how
much we progress in His service and praise when deprived of
such a bountiful pay, as it were, of consolations of special

graces."[51] Ignatius gives as the third reason for spiritual desolation: "He may give us a true knowledge whereby we may intimately feel that it is not in our power to acquire or retain
great devotion, ardent love, tears, or any other spiritual consolation, but that all is a gift and favour of God our Lord
. . . ."[52] This kind of desolation is clearly an exception.

When Hopkins' last sonnets are arranged so that the kind
of religious experience there reflected is paralleled with those
states of soul that Thomas a Kempis describes in his *Imitation
of Christ*, the similarity between the two is often quite close.
I have interjected Ignatius wherever I thought his points apply.
I have written the parallel in a kind of dialogue. The ex-
change is so dominated by Kempis and Hopkins that the impression is given that while these last poems are very much
within the Christian tradition of the spiritual life, they are the
least Ignatian. I do believe that some aspects of them, read in
the context of the total Hopkins canon while taking into
account their biographical implications, seem somewhat less Ignatian. The Ignatian discipline puts such heavy emphasis on
a psychic balance as the normal mental state, on consolation
as the normal spiritual state as means to true charity, that
this melancholic and desolate strain in Hopkins has to be put
down as not typically Ignatian nor, according to Ignatius himself, a desired inner disposition.

Hopkins begins:

> I wake and feel the fell of dark, not day.
> What hours, O what black hours we have spent
> This night! what sights you, heart, saw; ways you went!
> And more must, in yet longer light's delay.[53]

Kempis answers, "To suffer, therefore, is what awaits thee, if
thou art resolved to love Jesus, and constantly to serve Him.
. . . Know for certain that thou must lead a dying life, and
the more a man dieth to himself, the more doth he begin to
live unto God."[54]

Hopkins insists:

With witness I speak this. But where I say
Hours I mean years, mean life. And my lament
Is cries countless, cries like dead letters sent
To dearest him that lives alas! away.

Kempis answers, "O most miserable and foolish sinner, what
wilt thou answer unto God, Who knoweth all thine evil deeds
—thou who art afraid sometimes of an angry man?"[55] "For
our merit, and the advancement of our state, consists not in
having many sweetnesses and consolations; but rather in bear-
ing great afflictions and tribulations."[56]

Hopkins agrees:

I am gall, I am heartburn. God's most deep decree
Bitter would have me taste: my taste was me;
Bones built in me, flesh filled, blood brimmed the curse.
Selfyeast of spirit a dull dough sours. I see
The lost are like this, and their scourge to be
As I am mine, their sweating selves; but worse.

Kempis asks, "And how is it possible that the life of man can
be loved, which hath so great bitterness, and is subject to so
many calamities and miseries?"[57]

Hopkins cries:

No worst, there is none. Pitched past pitch of grief,
More pangs will, schooled at forepangs, wilder wring.
Comforter, where, where is your comforting?
Mary, mother of us, where is your relief?[58]

Kempis chides, "Where is thy faith? Stand firmly and persever-
ingly; practice endurance and manly courage; comfort will come
to thee in due season. [God is saying to you], 'Wait for Me, wait;
I will come and cure thee.' "[59]

Hopkins explains that he has pleaded:

My cries heave, herds-long; huddle in a main, a chief
Woe, world-sorrow; on an age-old anvil wince and
    sing—

> Then lull, then leave off. Fury had shrieked 'No ling-
> ering! Let me be fell; force I must be brief.'

Kempis explains, "It is good for us now and then to have some
troubles and adversities; for oftentimes they make a man enter
into himself, that he may know that he is an exile, and place
not his hopes in anything of the world."[60] "If it hath been
thus with great Saints, we that are weak and poor must not be
discouraged if we are sometimes fervent, sometimes cold, because the Spirit cometh and goeth according to His own
pleasure."[61]

Hopkins notes that not all men go to the depths of their
being as he has:

> O the mind, mind has mountains; cliffs of fall
> Frightful, sheer, no-man fathomed. Hold them cheap
> May who ne'er hung there. Nor does long our small
> Durance deal with that steep or deep. Here! creep,
> Wretch, under a comfort serves in a whirlwind: . . .

Kempis comments about man's plight, "For a long time shall
he be little, and lie grovelling beneath, who esteems anything
great but only the one, immense, eternal good."[62]

Ignatius, sensing infirmity, interrupts, "In time of desolation we must never make a change, but remain firm and constant in the resolutions and determination made on the day
preceding this desolation . . . ."[63] And Kempis advises biblically,
"I counsel thee to buy of Me gold tried in the fire, that thou
mayst become rich—that is heavenly wisdom, which treadeth
under foot all things below."[64] "For he is not worthy the sublime contemplation of God, who has not, for God's sake, been
exercised with some tribulation."[65] "And the higher a person
is advanced in spirit, the heavier crosses shall he often meet
with; because the pain of his banishment increaseth in pro-
portion to his love."[66]

Kempis bewails the lot of man, "I am poor, and in labors
from my youth, and my soul is saddened sometimes even unto
tears, and sometimes, too, my spirit is disturbed within herself
by reason of impending suffering."[67] "At such a time there is no

better remedy than patience, and denying of myself according to the will of God."[68]

Ignatius, who learned so much from Kempis, echoes his teacher: "Let him who is in desolation consider how our Lord, to try him, has left him to his natural powers, that he may resist the various agitations and temptations of the enemy; and to do so is always in his power, by the assistance of God, which always remains to him, though he may not clearly perceive it, as our Lord has withdrawn from him His great favour, great love and intense grace, leaving him, however, grace sufficient to his eternal salvation."[69] And he adds, "Let him who is in desolation strive to remain in patience, a virtue contrary to the troubles that harass him."[70]

Hopkins gains strength from his teachers:

Not, I'll not, carrion comfort, Despair, not feast on thee;
Not untwist—slack they may be—these last strands of man
In me ór, most weary, cry *I can no more.* I can;
Can something, hope, wish day come, not choose not to be.
But ah, but O thou terrible, why wouldst thou rude on me
Thy wring-world right foot rock? lay a lionlimb against me?
    scan
With darksome devouring eyes my bruisèd bones? and fan,
O in turns of tempest, me heaped there; me frantic to avoid
    thee and flee?[71]

Kempis explains in the name of the Lord, "I know thy most hidden thoughts, and that it is very expedient for thy salvation that thou sometimes be left without any savor of sweetness, lest perchance thou be puffed up with good success, and take complacency in thy self, imagining thyself to be what thou art not."[72] Rather one should say, "Thy discipline is upon me, and Thy rod itself shall instruct me."[73]

But Hopkins replies:

      THOU art indeed just, Lord, if I contend
      With thee; but, sir, so what I plead is just.
      Why do sinners' ways prosper? and why must
      Disappointment all I endeavor end?[74]

Kempis counters, "What I have given, I have power to take away, and restore as it pleases Me. . . . If I send thee affliction or any adversity, repine not, neither let thy heart be cast down. I can quickly raise thee up again, and turn all thy burden into joy. . . . If thou thinkest rightly, and considerest things in truth, thou oughtest never to be so much dejected and troubled at adversity. But thou shouldst rather rejoice and give thanks, yea, account this as a special subject of joy, that afflicting thee with sorrows I do not spare thee. . . . to bring forth much fruit in patience."[75]

But Hopkins sees all nature begetting:

>   See, banks and brakes
> Now, leavèd how thick! lacèd they are again
> With fretty chervil, look, and fresh wind shakes
> Them; birds build—but not I build; no, but strain,
> Time's eunuch, and not breed one work that wakes.
> Mine, O thou lord of life, send my roots rain.

Ignatius insists, "It belongs to God our Lord alone to grant consolation to the soul without any preceding cause for it, because it belongs to the Creator alone to go in and out of the soul, to excite motions in it, attracting it entirely to the love of His Divine Majesty."[76] Kempis adds, "When thou judgest that almost all is lost, then oftentimes it is that thou art in the way of the greatest gain of merit."[77] Putting himself in the role of the deity, he continues, "What is it thou sayest, My son? Cease to complain, and consider My Passion, and that of the other Saints. Thou hast not yet resisted unto blood."[78] "Be thou, therefore, prepared to fight, if thou desirest to gain the victory. Without conflict thou canst not attain the crown of patience."[79]

Hopkins understands:

> Why? That my chaff might fly; my grain lie, sheer and
>   clear.

Nay in all that toil, that coil, since (seems) I kissed the rod,
Hand rather, my heart lo! lapped strength, stole joy, would
    laugh, chéer.[80]

Kempis counsels as to the proper disposition of the desolate
heart by saying that one in such a state should pray, "Behold,
O beloved Father, I am in Thy Hands; I bow myself down under
the rod of Thy correction. Strike Thee my back and my neck,
that I may bind my perversity to Thy will."[81] "Lord, I am
not worthy of Thy consolation, nor of any spiritual visitation;
and, therefore, justly dost Thou deal with me, when Thou
leavest me poor and desolate."[82] "Lord, because Thou wast
patient in Thy lifetime, herein especially fulfilling the com-
mandment of Thy Father, it is fitting that I, a wretched sinner,
should, according to Thy will, bear myself patiently, and, as
long as Thou pleasest, support the burden of this corruptible
life, in order to gain my salvation."[83]
    Hopkins breaks in:

PATIENCE, hard thing! the hard thing but to pray,
But bid for, Patience is! Patience who asks
Wants war, wants wounds; weary his times, his tasks;
To do without, take tosses, and obey.
    Rare patience roots in these, and, these away, . . .

Kempis answers, pointing to the example of Christ, "Think not
thyself wholly forsaken, though for a time I have sent thee some
tribulation, or withdrawn from thee thy wished-for consolation;
for this is the way to the kingdom of heaven."[84] Like Christ,
"Dispose thyself to patience, rather than to consolations; and to
carrying the cross, rather than to gladness."[85] Hopkins affirms:

                He is patient. Patience fills
His crisp combs, and that comes those ways we know.[86]

But he can not live in this torment:

My own heart let me more have pity on; let
Me live to my sad self hereafter kind,
Charitable; not live this tormented mind
With this tormented mind tormenting yet.

I cast for comfort I can no more get
By groping round my comfortless, than blind
Eyes in their dark can day or thirst can find
Thirst's all-in-all in all a world of wet.

Kempis interrupts with practical advice, "When consolation
shall be taken away from thee, do not presently despair, but
with humility and patience await the heavenly visitation, since
God is able to restore to thee more abundant consolation."[87]
And Ignatius repeats, "It belongs to God our Lord alone to
grant consolation to the soul . . . ."[88] Hopkins understands:

Soul, self; come, poor Jackself, I do advise
You, jaded, let be; call off thoughts awhile
Elsewhere; leave comfort root-room; let joy size
At God knows when to God knows what; whose smile
's not wrung, see you; unforseen times rather—as skies
Betweenpie mountains—lights a lovely mile.[89]

This "sheer plod" love will cause, continues Hopkins:

Flesh fade, and mortal trash
Fall to the residuary worm; world's wildfire, leave but ash:

And Ignatius and Kempis join with him:

In a flash, at a trumpet crash,
I am all at once what Christ is, since he was what I am, and
This Jack, joke, poor potsherd, patch, matchwood, immortal
diamond,
Is immortal diamond.

This dialogue shows that the so-called "terrible sonnets"
which Hopkins wrote during the last years of his life are meaningful in the light of Christian asceticism. The sonnets, when

juxtaposed with the *Spiritual Exercises* and *The Imitation of Christ,* are not just Freudian manifestations of frustration, if indeed they are that at all, but they are the revelations of a spiritual plight the result of which God alone knows. They reveal the anguish and the joy of spirit which the writings of all the saints, mystical and otherwise, bear witness to. This is not to say that Hopkins was a mystic or that these are mystical poems. It is to say that they are poems of a devout man who suffered periods of intense spiritual desolation similar to those experienced by the saints. Moreover, there is no question that his physical anemia played a large part in his distress. Nevertheless, there is a consonance between the kind of experience described in the long tradition of Christian asceticism (which includes, of course, the Spiritual Exercises) and those experiences related in these poems. This would suggest that a large measure of their significance lies in Christian theology.

At the same time, these sonnets must be seen in their proper context within the total canon of Hopkins. Viewed in this perspective, there is apparent throughout the canon, as Dixon observed, a "terrible pathos" which the last sonnets exhibit in its greatest intensity. Hopkins' poems are filled with the fear of the Lord. He expresses again and again the significance of God as against the insignificance of man. To him, the difference is a terrible one, especially when man acts as if there were none, or at most a very slight one. At first sight, it would seem that this dwelling on the Old Testament God of Justice is not only antithetical to Ignatius, but also is unchristian. It is neither, according to Ignatius. In an addition to the Spiritual Exercises under the title, "Rules for thinking with the Church," there is stated what amounts to the traditional Christian attitude: "Although it is above all things praiseworthy to greatly serve God our Lord out of pure love, yet we ought much to praise the fear of His Divine Majesty, because not only is filial fear a pious and most holy thing, but even servile fear, when a man does not rise to anything better and more useful, is of great help to him to escape from mortal sin; and, after he has escaped from it, he easily attains to filial fear, which is altogether acceptable and pleasing to God our Lord, because it is inseparable from Divine love."[91] Evidently Hopkins' attitude is not heterodox nor un-Ignatian. Yet it ought to be noted that his emphasis on fear is not typically Ignatian. There is a definite progression in the Spiritual Exercises from the First Week when Ignatius confronts the exercitant with fear of the God of Justice to the Fourth Week when he substitutes love as the prime motive of Christian action. And this progression is an essential one in the Ignatian discipline.

Hopkins does seem to dwell unduly on the First Week in his poetry.[92] But this makes sense in Hopkins' case. Every Jesuit personalizes Ignatius for himself. It is apparent that in his earliest writing, especially the jottings in his notebooks, that his moral sensibility was very acute. His spiritual notebooks of the Anglican period contain lists of sins to be confessed which indicate how tender and sensitive his conscience was. And his conversion to Catholicism probably intensified this in him. By the time that he had been taught Ignatius' bookkeeping method of examining one's conscience, surely this tendency would have become even stronger. Moreover, the first two facts with which Ignatius confronts the new exercitant are God's justice and fear of damnation because of personal sin. This must have made a very deep impression on a young man, a convert, who before he was so confronted already had taken them with a degree of seriousness that was unusually intense. It is not surprising, then, that Hopkins with his scrupulous turn of mind often gave expression to his feeling of terrible nothingness of self and the overwhelming all of God.

However, it would be a mistake to think that Hopkins' poetry never got to the contemplative love of the Fourth Week. The Ignatian progression is unmistakably there.[93] Even the bitterest moments of the "terrible" sonnets are unmarked by anything like despair. The most "terrible" sonnet of the lot, whatever one chooses, is offset by poems written at approximately the same time which are full of consolation and love. Hopkins put the whole matter in one line in "The Wreck of the Deutschland": "Thou art lightning and love, I found it, a winter and warm."

There is a page in the Dublin notebook (August or September, 1884) which elucidates every poem that Hopkins ever wrote. This page was written when both his health and his work were bringing him to a terrible spiritual despondency. It was "Time's eunuch" writing:

"Man was created to praise etc

"Praise by the office expressly meant for this; by the mass, especially the Gloria

"And the other things on earth—take it that weakness, ill health, every cross is a help. Calix quem Pater meus dedit mihi non bibam illud?

"Facere nos indifferentes—with the elective will, not the affective essentially; but the affective will will follow

"I must ask God to strengthen my faith or I shall never keep the particular examen. I must say the stations for this intention.

Resolve also to keep it particularly even in the present state of lethargy

. . . .

"Consider how the Bd. Virgin praises God, her obedience, sorrows, her prayer, her work, her holy death

"Rejoice in her glory. Consider the meeting between Christ and his mother and how the joy of seeing Christ our Lord is from having lived for him. Pray therefore earnestly to do this

"Consider the particular examen and the prayers for it; also rules of modesty

"Foundation—Exercise

"Man was created—Here consider what Father D. M. was talking about

"Save his soul—Consider in this life the meaning of these words.

Consider peace, contentment, a good conscience

"And the other things—Resolve how to get more use of them

"Man was created—Say the man Christ was created to praise etc and to save his soul, that is/enter into his glory.

And the other things as in his train

"The love of the Son for the Father leads him to take a created nature and in that to offer him sacrifice. The

sacrifice might have been unbloody: by the Fall it became a bloody one"[94]

Humphry House, the first editor of Hopkins' *Note-Books and
Papers,* describes the last sentences of the passage as follows:
"In the last sentences he stopped on the word 'created' and
wrote it again, twice the size, in a huge, sprawling, childlike
hand; crossed it out, began again 'cr' still bigger; crossed that
out too, and in the same hand wrote 'crea.' That was in Dublin,
August or September 1884; and the next page is completely
filled with /'s, made as he marked the papers."[95]

HOMO CREATUS EST LAUDARE.   Mr. House comments
on this sentence in a way that fittingly sums up the interpretation of Hopkins, the man and poet, that is being suggested in
this book:

> No single sentence better explains the motives and
> direction of Hopkins's life than this "Man was created
> to praise." He believed it as wholly as a man can believe
> anything; and when regret or sorrow over anything in
> his life comes to a critic's mind this must be remem-
> bered. To remember it is not to share or advocate the
> belief; but it is essential to an intelligent reading of
> his work.[96]

Ignatius called spiritual consolation an excitement in the soul
of "some interior motion by which it begins to be inflamed
with the love of its Creator and Lord, and when, consequently,
it can love no created thing on the face of the earth in itself,
but only in the Creator of them all."[97] This explains Mr.
House's observation about Hopkins, for Hopkins knew of what
Ignatius named the "call of Christ," and in his own life experienced a measure of what Ignatius experienced, that desolation of self that all sacred history records as the victory that
often must be won if praise is to be given.

CHAPTER SIX

Hopkins and the Meditative Tradition

"The world is charged with the grandeur of God."

This study has thus far examined the Ignatian content of
Hopkins' poetry. It is now possible to turn to some of the
esthetic implications of the Ignatian method of meditation as
they apply to Hopkins' art. The Ignatian method of prayer
does have esthetic implications. Surely Ignatius' directions to
the exercitant to see "with the eyes of the imagination" is not
only a prescription for imaginative prayer. It may serve as a
description of the poetic imagination. Some poetry can be
described as meditations having moral, allegorical, and anagogical implications. Such poetry is verbal reconstruction of
interior dispositions which are the result of experience perceived as having moral, or allegorical, or anagogical meanings
and significances. When one is trained to confront certain experiences in this manner for purposes of meditative prayer, it
can be seen how the meditating mind can be led astray into
phantasms that distract from efficacious prayer. Ignatius knew
this and thus insisted that the reflection pass on from the
imagination to the intellect. On the other hand, if the reflection
delays in the imagination, though this might frustrate an act
of prayer, it may well generate an act of poetry. Whether it is
good poetry or not depends on whether a poet has interrupted
his prayer. The important point is that Ignatian prayer and
meditative poetry do begin on the sensuous level, that though in
both there is a passage to other levels, nevertheless in both the
soul draws its delight and profit through the sensible. Perhaps
this can best be seen by examining the structure of the Ignatian

meditation, and then examining some of Hopkins' poetry for parallel structural relationships.

The Ignatian meditation is made of three basic elements. The first is the notable "composition of place, seeing the spot." Here, it will be recalled, the exercitant is directed to re-create in his imagination in rich detail the whole matter of the meditation. Ignatius directs the exercitant over and over again to form concrete images of the matter of his meditation, no matter how abstract. This basic part could be performed in one of three ways. The first is to imagine oneself in the actual place where the event ocurred. The second is to dramatize the events as they happened "in the very same place where you are." The third, the most difficult of the three, is to imagine the events as taking place within one's own soul.

Now this intense and deliberate attention to the imaginative re-creation of the meditative matter is clearly parallel to the image-making in the poetic process. In his study of meditative poetry, Professor Martz sees this lying behind the vivid and dramatic quality of so much of the religious poetry of the seventeenth century. In making this point, he specifically directs our attention to the openings of some of John Donne's "Holy Sonnets." No one can deny that the openings of some of them are "grand and passionate." It is no less true for Hopkins:

The World is charged with the grandeur of God.

. . . .

Look at the stars! look, look up at the skies!

. . . .

I caught this morning morning's minion, . . .

. . . .

Earnest, earthless, equal, attuneable, vaulty, volumi-
    nous, . . stupendous
Evening . . .

. . . .

As kingfishers catch fire, dragonflies draw flame;

. . . .

Not, I'll not, carrion comfort, Despair not feast on thee;
.   .   .   .

No worst, there is none, Pitched past pitch of grief,
More pangs will, schooled at forepangs, wilder wring.
.   .   .   .

I wake and feel the fell of dark, not day.
.   .   .   .

As a dare-gale skylark scanted in a dull cage
Man's mounting spirit in his bone-house, mean house,
      dwells—
.   .   .   .

Thou mastering me
God!
.   .   .   .

Thou art indeed just, Lord, if I contend
With Thee;

Now in Hopkins' case, these richly sensuous moments are insights into Infinite Being because of the very process of sensation. Hopkins, seconded by Scotus, held the notion that previous to consciousness, man has a kind of sensation which fleetingly envisions nature uncorrupted leading to a perception of flashing intimations of Infinite Being. This is the beginning of awareness which quickly passes into consciousness. Hopkins experienced this spiritualization of sense experience before he confirmed it in the speculations of Scotus, for his earliest writings show beneath his reveling in sense experience a gradual process of spiritualization. His early concern for revitalizing the surfeiting senses was mainly esthetic, serving as a springboard into a search of religion for whatever aid it might proffer. The path he followed is well known.

Neither is the drama of these and other passages purely the result of an arbitrary artistic execution, but rather one which derived from this process of visionary sensation. As a poet, he was concerned in capturing these flashes of truth in all their beauty. Somehow poetic form had to record both the flash of sense and the intense attendant sensations in order that they might be affixed as actions dramatically expressed. Moreover, there was the poet's own response and reaction to his experience which also had to seep into the gestures of his language. Hopkins' poems invariably express this extension of that first, fresh sight which dramatically leads through the finite to a glimpse of the Infinite which insight moves the poet's heart: "I walk, I lift up heart, eyes,/Down all that glory in the heavens to glean our Saviour; . . . which two when they meet,/The heart rears wings bold and bolder/And hurls for him, O half hurls earth for him off under his feet."

Perhaps this fusion of his and Scotus' views of human psychology with Ignatius' meditative method of "seeing with the eyes of the imagination" is the most profound influence on Hopkins' art. The characteristic configuration of his poetry has been described by more than one reader as sensation, intuition, and response. This pattern bears too close a resemblance to the general design of the Ignatian meditation (in which the mediative matter is vividly imagined, the senses being used to personalize the scene, and the intellect and will in turn make inferences and draw forth affections), for the parallels to be a coincidence, as further consideration will show.

The second element of the Ignatian meditation is the use of "the three powers." The memory is used to recall distinctly the matter of the meditation; the understanding is to study and consider the mystery; the will is to use the intellectual analysis as a means to draw forth virtuous attitudes, affections, and acts. This trinity of human powers is analogous to the Holy Trinity. Theologians see all sorts of implications in the analogy. In meditation, for example, man employs this trinity to elevate and renew his fallen nature so that he will be truly in the image of God. This state of soul is the goal of all meditation. An excellent statement of the human trinity of powers and its relationship to the Divine Trinity is made by the philosopher, Étienne Gilson, in his commentary on St. Bonaventure:

Just as the father engenders the eternal knowledge
of the Word Who expresses Him, and as the Word is
in turn united with the Father by the Holy Spirit,

so memory or thought, big with ideas which it encloses, engenders the knowledge of the intellect or word, and love is born from both as the bond which unites them. It is no accidental correspondence that is here described; the structure of the creative Trinity conditions and therefore explains the structure of the human soul.[1]

The third element of the Ignatian meditation is the culmination of the meditation, the colloquy. It will be recalled that this is a free interchange between God and man in which each converses with the other, as servant, friend, and loved one. It is a council of love. Jesuit commentators, in talking about the colloquy, expand it in vivid dramatic detail. It should be noted that these three elements follow one another in a unified sequence: composition, analysis, and colloquy. The "three powers" unify the meditation: the memory composes the meditation; the intellect analyzes it; the will elicits affections and virtuous acts in the colloquy.

These three elements of the Ignatian meditation ought to be apparent in the writing of a poet who was fully acquainted with the Ignatian method of meditation, and whose total body poetic is primarily religious. It ought to be apparent, that is, if his meditative experience informed in some way his poetic practice. These three elements are in Hopkins' poetry. In most poems, they are rather generally reflected as the pattern of experience; some, and they are significant in number, amount almost to a poetic version of a spiritual exercise. "Spelt from Sibyl's Leaves,"[2] one of Hopkins' most studied and praised sonnets, is a good example of the triple structure of the Ignatian exercise poeticized.

The sonnet falls into three distinct sections which closely resemble the three meditative structures. In the first part, the poet (he could be called the exercitant) composes in vivid and dramatic detail an occurrence in nature:

EARNEST, earthless, equal, attuneable, vaulty, voluminous, . .
    stupendous
Evening strains to be time's vast, womb-of-all, home-of-all,
    hearse-of-all night.

Her fond yellow hornlight wound to the west, her wild
    hollow hoarlight hung to the height
Waste; her earliest stars, earl-stars, stárs principal, overbend us,
Fíre-féaturing heaven. For earth her being has unbound, her
    dapple is at an end, as-
tray or aswarm, all throughther, in throngs; self ín self steepèd
    and páshed—qúite
Disremembering, dísmémbering áll now.

The poet narrates the end of day and the advent of night. His
primary subject of description is evening: "Evening strains to
be . . . night." The speaker's composition is first, "Fire-featur-
ing heaven." Then he composes the earth as it appears to him
at the time of this happening. The dominant motif is oblivion:
"her being has unbound."

The second section corresponds to the meditative structure
of analysis. Here the poet in the true spirit of meditation looks
deep into the event he has composed to discover the hidden
meanings that must lie there for him in the mystery of nature.
His study of the event results in his seeing the natural event
of evening as a terrifying symbol of his own destructive death:

                                Heart you round
    me right
With: Óur évening is over us; óur night whélms, whélms,
    ánd will end us.
Only the beak-leaved boughs dragonish damask the tool-
    smooth bleak light; black,
Ever so black on it.

The third section can be considered a colloquy. Here the
speaker becomes silent to listen to the divine warning in his
heart that all shall be reduced to the universal simplicity of
right and wrong, and he is urged to be earnestly concerned
with these two: "mind/But these two." Further, he is warned
that the world is indifferent to these two, that the world does not
resolve into right and wrong. Finally, the poetic colloquy ends
with the admonishment to avoid trying to live a life, as it
were, between right and wrong, for this is to be put on a
frightful rack of suffering. Here is the last section:

Óur tale, O óur oracle! Lét life, wáned,
 ah lét life wind
Off hér once skéined stained véined variéty upon, áll on two
 spools; párt, pen, páck
Now her áll in twó flocks, twó folds—black, white; right, wrong;
 reckon but, reck but, mind
But thése two; wáre of a wórld where bút these twó tell, each
 off the óther; of a rack
Where, selfwrung, selfstrung, sheathe- and shelterless, thóughts
 agaínst thoughts ín groans grínd.

This sonnet, I submit, closely resembles in structure the
triple structure of the Ignatian meditation. There is a "seeing
of the spot," (in the normal Ignatian tradition, it will be recalled, of beginning with created nature), an analysis of the hidden meanings, real and symbolical, of the event composed, and,
finally, an earnest exhortation to the exercitant, in oracular
fashion, to heed the divine whispers which he hears in his
heart. Moreover, the total poetic content is meditative matter,
the poetic tone reflective. It is hard to find a poem more central
in the tradition of meditative poetry.

Even a lesser poem such as "Pied Beauty,"[3] shows how deeply
the meditative structure and spirit of the Ignatian spiritual
exercise informed Hopkins' poetic matter: "Glory be to God
for dappled things—" The poet then composes the matter in
rich detail:

For skies of couple-colour as a brinded cow;
 For rose-moles all in stipple upon trout that swim;
Fresh-firecoal chestnut-falls; finches' wings;
 Landscape plotted and pieced—fold, fallow, and plough;
 And all trades, their gear and tackle and trim.

All things counter, original, spare, strange;
 Whatever is fickle, freckled (who knows how?)
 With swift, slow; sweet, sour; adazzle, dim;

The next to the last line is a brief but incisive analysis of the
composed matter: "He fathers-forth whose beauty is past change."
The last abbreviated doxology is an excellent Ignatian colloquy:

"Praise him." To be sure, this poem because of its swift inductive ascent, resembles the meditative structure less than the foregoing poem; still, I think, its influence is here.

It has been pointed out that the triple structure of the spiritual exercise is in formal accord with the 4-4-6 division of the traditional Petrarchan sonnet. Such sonnets possibly offer historically the best poetic examples of the influences of the meditative tradition on religious poetry of a reflective nature. This is certainly true of Hopkins' Petrarchan sonnets, for example, his famous sonnet, "The Windhover,"[4] which is virtually a transfiguration of Ignatius' meditation on the Kingdom of Christ.

In the octave of this sonnet, the Jesuit poet composes the pomp and circumstance of "daylight's dauphin," with the result that he is deeply stirred by the superb performance of the creature:

I CAUGHT this morning morning's minion, king-
 dom of daylight's dauphin, dapple-dawn-drawn Falcon, in
  his riding
Of the rolling level underneath him steady air, and striding
High there, how he rung upon the rein of a wimpling wing
In his ecstasy! then off, off forth on swing,
 As a skate's heel sweeps smooth on a bow-bend: the hurl
  and gliding
 Rebuffed the big wind. My heart in hiding
Stirred for a bird,—the achieve of, the mastery of the thing!

The opening line has that dramatic power we have come to associate with meditative poetry. Here, as before, the poet perceives the striking beauty of the "place." He is inwardly taken with the beauty of creation. He has two necessary meditative dispositions: an intense imaginative image, and a deep involvement in it. The imagination has seen the spot.

In the sestet, the second and third structures of the meditative exercise are reversed. The affections elicited by the will precede the intellectual perception. However, this is of no consequence since Ignatius (as well as his commentators) always makes clear that in the Exercises these structures are most flexible in both sequence and length. He warns in a number of places that the Exercises are fully adaptable to the spiritual needs of the exercitant. In the first lines of the sestet, the will of the poet, in his realization of the Master behind the mastery of creation, is moved to an act of sacrifice:

Brute beauty and valour and act, oh, air, pride, plume, here
    Buckle!

The poet wills abnegation of "mortal beauty." The intellect enhances and supports the will act as an act of "immortal beauty" in the remaining lines of the sestet. It is interesting here that the meditative poet reaches the poetic climax not in the affections of the colloquy, but in the analysis of the second power:[5]

AND the fire that breaks from thee then, a billion
Times told lovelier, more dangerous, O my chevalier!

    No wonder of it: shéer plód makes plough down sillion
Shine, and blue-bleak embers, ah my dear,
    Fall, gall themselves, and gash gold-vermillion.

Another one of Hopkins' Petrarchan sonnets bears remarkable resemblance to the structure of the Ignatian meditation. This is the one entitled, "God's Grandeur."[6] The sonnet opens with a dramatic assertion, an announcement of the meditative matter: "The world is charged with the grandeur of God." The octave continues with a highly imaginative illumination of this assertion which is then set against the way the world fares under man's "charge":

    It will flame out, like shining from shook foil;
    It gathers to a greatness, like the ooze of oil
Crushed. Why do men then now not reck his rod?
Generations have trod, have trod, have trod;
    And all is seared with trade; bleared, smeared with toil;
    And wears man's smudge and shares man's smell; the soil
Is bare now, nor can foot feel, being shod.

In the sestet, the lines move from the study of the intellect to the creative love of the Holy Spirit in the colloquy. The intellect discovers that somehow nature stays fresh no matter how man-blighted; in searching for the reason, it discerns that God in the Third Person is still "charging" the world. In the last two lines, we have what may be called a colloquy in which the Holy Spirit communicates to the "bent/World" its regenerative powers, a message of Divine Love:

And for this, nature is never spent;
There lives the dearest freshness deep down things;
And though the last lights off the black West went
Oh, morning, at the brown brink eastward, springs—
Because the Holy Ghost over the bent
World broods with warm breast and with ah! bright wings.

This sort of movement in Hopkins' poetry, from the creature to the Creator, from the natural to the supernatural, is highly consonant with the Ignatian vision and admirably suited to the formal structures of the sonnet form. The very structures of the Ignatian exercise seem well suited to the artistic principle of the sonnet, a poetic form that meditative poets have made much use of. The total motion and structure of many of Hopkins' sonnets resemble the triple structural pattern of the meditative exercise much too closely for it to be accidental. And the fact of his Jesuit priesthood is tantamount to certain and definite Ignatian meditative influences on his writing both in form and matter.

The poems I have examined are not the only ones subject to profitable examination from this vantage point. Such poems as "The Starlight Night," "Spring," "The Lantern Out of Doors," "The Sea and the Skylark," "The Caged Skylark," "The Candle Indoors," "Ribblesdale," "The Leaden Echo and the Golden Echo," and "Thou art indeed Just, Lord" are all in the meditative tradition, and bear important relationships to the structure of the Ignatian spiritual exercise. More could be added to the list. However, the overriding fact in all these poems is that they are artistic reflections of the ascent of human consciousness to divinity as well as poetic records of the highest of human aspirations, an act of perfect love. Meditation is a prelude to love of God. Hopkins, as only the artist can, affixed this ecstatic climb of the human spirit within the conservation of art, which, unfortunately, he could not look on as his prelude to love.

There is another facet of the Ignatian spiritual exercise which can be shown to have had some influence on Hopkins' poetry. It has been pointed out that Christ is the central meditative matter of the Spiritual Exercises. Further, it has been noted that the chief aim of all meditations on the life of Christ is to realize, at once, the divinity and humanity of Christ. The purpose of this aim is the elevation of one's human nature until it becomes a perfect mirror of the divine. The chief means to this end is commemoration of the Christian mysteries, especially the sacrificial commemoration of the Passion, Death, and Resurrection. This commemoration takes more than one form. It may be meditative commemoration which we are concerned with here. It may be by actually experiencing, willfully or accidentally, situations paralleling the Christian mysteries as acts of commemoration. All of these means are common to Christian usage.

Ignatius wrote a sequence of five exercises of meditation on the life of Christ. Unlike the First Week, he wrote three preludes (instead of two) by which he emphasized the necessity for detailed "composition of place." The first four exercises are to be performed by means of the three powers of the soul. The fifth exercise, however, marks a departure. Here Ignatius, it will be recalled, directs the exercitant to apply his senses to the matter of the foregoing exercises. He is to "see the persons," "hear what they are saying," "smell and taste the infinite sweetness and delight of the Divinity," feel with the touch; "as, for example, to kiss and embrace the spots where such persons tread and sit." The effect of such an exercise is to fuse the three powers (directed at the life of Christ) into an intense and intricate experience, such that its psychological impact be of the kind which causes significant and, often, radical change in the exercitant. This emphasis on realization very probably lies behind Hopkins' dramatic use of verbs of apprehension (look, see, catch, lift, flash, crash), and of response (master, have, get, buy, bid), to mention but a few.

The artistic implications of such meditative experiences for the religious poet are many. The ample use of the imagination, the force of the experience on the senses, the complex fusion of the three powers, indeed the total impact of the experience parallel the nature of the poetic act. Possibly, there is identity of action with only the intention of each distinguishing the nature of the act as religious or artistic. At least for Hopkins, it is possible to so argue.

Hopkins" sonnet, "Hurrahing in Harvest,"[7] exhibits something very much like Ignatius' famous "application of senses." In this poem, the poet exults over discovering in the beauty of nature the beauty of Christ.[8] The sonnet opens with a dramatic description of harvest:

Summer ends now; now, barbarous in beauty, the stocks arise
　Around; up above, what wind-walks! what lovely
　　behaviour
　Of silk-sack clouds! has wilder, wilful-wavier
Meal-drift moulded ever and melted across skies?

In the next lines, the poet through the triple powers of his soul discovers the Saviour in the beauty of Nature's harvest. He then re-examines this natural beauty in the light of its supernatural significance. In doing so, he invokes the senses to see, hear, and feel the divine Christ in natural reality. The poem ends in an ecstasy of colloquy in which the poet pictures "the beholder" leaping up to his God "when once they meet":

I walk, I lift up heart, eyes,
　Down all that glory in the heavens to glean our Saviour;
　And, éyes, heárt, what looks, what lips yet gave you a
Rapturous love's greeting of realer, of rounder replies?

And the azurous hung hills are his world-wielding shoulder
　Majestic—as a stallion stalwart, very-violet-sweet!—
These things, these things were here and but the beholder
　Wanting; which two when they once meet,

The heart rears wings bold and bolder
And hurls for him, O half hurls earth for him off under
    his feet.

This fusion of intense feeling and thought, of theological
abstraction and sense experience,[9] so ordered that the structure
reaches a climax in which Christ, God and man, is simultaneously comprehended and concretely felt with overwhelming
impact, is a description of the goal of the Ignatian meditation
on the life of Christ. It could also serve as a critical description of the foregoing sonnet. The similarity is more than an
accident. Meditative method has decidedly informed poetic act.

This sort of complex fusion occurs often in Hopkins' poetry,
if not to the extent of a total reflection of the meditative structure of the Ignatian exercise on the life of Christ, then at those
parts of poems where Christ enters into the poetic content. This
is apparent in the sestet of the sonnet we have already examined,
"The Windhover," in which the poet fuses with passion the
concept of sacrifice for love of Christ with the concrete image
of plowing, so that through verbal figures he conveys the theological concept of the worth of an act, and his admiration for it.

The same sort of fusion takes place in "The Wreck of the
Deutschland."[10] I have already suggested that the configuration
of this poem resembles in many ways the total structure of the
Spiritual Exercises as Hopkins understood and experienced
them. It can be suggested further that in many places in this
poem the type of union we have been discussing can be found,
for we find theological doctrine passionately expressed in
climactic structures of the most sensuous imagery. The last two
stanzas of Part I provide good examples:

        Be adored among men
      God, three-numberèd form;
    Wring thy rebel, dogged in den,
      Man's malice, with wrecking and storm.
    Beyond saying sweet, past telling of tongue,
Thou art lightning and love, I have found it, a winter and warm;

Father and fondler of heart thou hast wrung:
Hast thy dark descending and most art merciful then.

With an anvil-ding
And with fire in him forge thy will
Or, rather then, stealing as Spring
Through him, melt him but master him still:
Whether at once, as once at a crash Paul,
Or as Austin, a lingering-out swéet skíll,
Make mercy in all of us, out of us all
Mastery, but be adored, but be adored King.

Though I will not quote them, stanzas 5, 8, 22, 30, 32-35 of the same poem all contain a similar kind of fusion which has notable affinity with the Ignatian meditation on the life of Christ, especially the application of senses. The tension of such religious poetry is too parallel to the experiences of the Ignatian meditation to be accidental, particularly for the Jesuit Hopkins.

Parts of other poems can be noted. The kind of union that takes place in the sonnet, "God's Grandeur" is a type which is similar to the Ignatian application of the senses. The use of the sunset and dawn coupled with the image of the Holy Spirit as a bird setting on the world as a nest, represents most concretely the role of the Third Person of the Trinity as theologians conceive it, as well as the poet's feeling providential security.

Another example, possibly even more striking, is the sestet of the sonnet, "As kingfishers catch fire."[11] After having declared in the octave his doctrine of the unique quality of all being and its tendency to enunciate its "self," Hopkins fuses his doctrine of "self" with the Incarnation. This union is managed poetically in imagery which pictures man reflecting Christ in his very being. But it is more than reflection. It is a union of man and God. Here Hopkins anticipated a modern theological emphasis, that of the doctrine of the Mystical Body—another instance of his theological brilliance—which emphasizes the infiltration of grace in human nature. This is Hopkins' statement of the mystical body of Christ:

I say more: the just man justices;
Keeps grace: that keeps all his goings graces;
Acts in God's eye what in God's eye he is—
Christ—for Christ plays in ten thousand places
Lovely in limbs, and lovely in eyes not his
To the Father through the features of men's faces.

There remains yet another type of meditation to examine for its esthetic implications. This is the sort which has been called meditations of spiritual communion. Christian meditative literature is from the beginning replete with communion meditations. They range from the simple mental re-enactment of some sort of communion service to the richly liturgical eucharistic sacrifice of a solemn high mass. The colloquy, of course, is a kind of spiritual communion.

Hopkins described the Holy Eucharist in his joyous poem, "The Bugler's First Communion,"[12] as "Low-latched in leaflight housel his too huge godhead." However, the majority of his poems of the Jesuit period celebrate spiritual communion with Christ rather than explicit communion services of the Church. Possibly his most successful poetic statement of spiritual communion comes at the close of his sonnet, "That Nature is a Heraclitean Fire and of the comfort of the Resurrection."[13] In the first part of the poem, he stated that nature moves on and on while "her bonniest, dearest to her, her clearest-selvèd spark Man . . . is gone!" This takes the poet into bleak dejection until he recalls the significance of the Resurrection. Because of man's spiritual communion with Christ, because by Christ becoming man, man becomes Christ, becomes immortal, the poet is raised from the depths of despair to the elation of spiritual joy. Hopkins attempts to poetically express both the theological meaning of Easter as well as its emotional impact by fusing an abstract idea (immortality) to a concrete object which is very precious (diamond). The result is a tense fusion, akin to the sort of union already mentioned, which poetically captures the startling implications for man of his spiritual communion with the Incarnate Christ. Here is the section:

> Across my foundering deck shone
> A beacon, an eternal beam. Flesh fade, and mortal trash
> Fall to the residuary worm; world's wildfire, leave but ash:
> In a flash, at a trumpet crash,
> I am all at once what Christ is, since he was what I am, and
> This Jack, joke, poor potsherd, patch, matchwood, immortal
>   diamond,
> Is immortal diamond.

There is also another form of meditation based on communion with Christ. This is meditation on Christ with the Virgin Mary as mediatrix. These meditations were fostered primarily by devotion to the Virgin, and were often based on the methodical prayer systems of the rosary. Devotion to the Virgin has been always a special concern of the Jesuits; they fostered it during the Counter Reformation and have cultivated it to this very day. The Virgin appears over and over again in Hopkins' poetry; however, these poems which are written specifically about her show little or no influence from the rosary. They are devotional rather than meditative pieces emphasizing her role as the Mother of God, and thus a mediatrix for all men. The poem, "Rosa Mystica,"[14] for example, examines the implications of this epithet from the Litany of the Virgin:

> Tell me the name now, tell me its name:
> The heart guesses easily, is it the same?
> Mary, the Virgin, well the heart knows,
> She is the Mystery, she is that Rose.

The same is true of the poem, "The May Magnificat."[15] In this rhythmic poem he relates that "May is Mary's month":

> This ecstasy all through mothering earth
> Tells Mary her mirth till Christ's birth
> To remember and exultation
> In God who was her salvation.

Another poem to Mary, however, is something more than devotional. This is, "The Blessed Virgin compared to the Air we Breathe."[16] Here the theme is communion with Christ through Mary, again a typical theological and meditative subject; however, Hopkins' poetic management of it amounts to a kind of meditation. He states that just as the "Wild air, world —mothering air" sustains man's life, so the immaculate nature of the Virgin is the sweet atmosphere through which God came to man and still comes to man:

> This air, which by life's law,
> My lung must draw and draw
> Now but to breathe its praise,
> Minds me in many ways
> Of her who not only
> Gave God's infinity
> Dwindled to infancy
> Welcome in womb and breast,
> Birth, milk, and all the rest
> But mothers each new grace
> That does now reach our race—

Mary "mantles the guilty globe":

> I say that we are wound
> With mercy round and round
> As if with air: the same
> Is Mary, more by name.

It is through her that Christ is born anew in each man:[17]

> If I have understood,
> She holds high motherhood
> Towards all our ghostly good
> And plays in grace her part
> About man's beating heart,
> Laying, like air's fine flood,
> The deathdance in his blood;
> Yet no part but what will
> Be Christ our Saviour still.
> Of her flesh he took flesh:
> He does take fresh and fresh,
> Though much the mystery how,

> Not flesh but spirit now
> And makes, O marvellous!
> New Nazareths in us,
> Where she shall yet conceive
> Him, morning, noon, and eve;
> New Bethlems, and he born
> There, evening, noon, and morn—

The poem ends in a kind of colloquy with the Virgin in which Hopkins fuses his figure with the insight in such a way that the total poetic structure is neatly closed:

> Be thou then, O thou dear
> Mother, my atmosphere;
> My happier world, wherein
> To wend and meet no sin;
> Above me, round me lie
> Fronting my froward eye
> With sweet and scarless sky;
> Stir in my ears, speak there
> Of God's love, O live air,
> Of patience, penance, prayer:
> World-mothering air, air wild,
> Wound with thee, in thee isled,
> Fold home, fast fold thy child.

This brief study has indicated, I trust, that the methods of Ignatian meditation are very much akin to the creative processes of the imagination, and this being so, had considerable artistic influence on Hopkin's poetry. While it is true that few poems amount to a shortened or condensed meditation of the sort that is found in the Spiritual Exercises, nevertheless the total configuration of many of Hopkins' poems has such correspondence with the structure of the Ignatian meditation, that it can hardly be denied that methodical meditative patterns influenced his poetry. And Hopkins' background warrants my specifying them as Ignatian, though the conclusive evidence is the poems themselves, which I have tried to show as substantiating this contention.

We have seen that Hopkins' poetic content is primarily re-

ligious. We have seen that his poetic tone is meditative. We now
see that his poetic style is meditative. Mr. Louis Martz, in his
fine study of meditative poetry, fashioned a definition of meditative style which is made up of concepts and terminology
which he drew largely from Hopkins. It serves quite satisfactorily
as a description of Hopkins' meditative style: "Meditative style,
then, is 'current language heightened,' molded, to express the
unique being of an individual who has learned, by intense
mental discipline, to live his life in the presence of divinity."[18]
He sees this style as belonging to Donne, Herbert, Vaughan,
Crashaw, Marvell; he finds it in Southwell, Edward Taylor,
Blake, Wordsworth, Hopkins, Emily Dickinson, Yeats' later
poetry and also Eliot's. He further states, "It is a style that may
in places permeate the drama, the epic, the narrative poem,
and of course the forms of prose as well. Hamlet speaks his
meditations; *Paradise Lost* presents in Book VII a formal meditation on Genesis; *Paradise Regained* displays a muted ground-
style related to the meditative, for the whole poem is, in some
degree, a meditation on the life of Christ. One might speak,
too, of certain writers who approach a meditative style at
times: Tennyson in *In Memoriam,* or Wallace Stevens in his
later poetry. And it is, surely, a style that may be found in other
ages, other lands, and other languages; in our own century we
find the style in Rilke, Claudel, and Peguy."[19]

Mr. Martz described his effort as an attempt "to discern a
genre, to suggest that, as we speak of the Petrarchan, the
pastoral, the epic, or the mock heroic, so too we might speak
of the meditative."[20] If he has been successful, and I think he
has, then Hopkins was a traditionalist writing within the
meditative genre. Moreover, he was a traditionalist who wrote
with that true sense of the historical, which Mr. T. S. Eliot
has defined as "a sense of the timeless as well as of the temporal
and of the timeless and the temporal together." By the delayed
publication of his verse, he was made a twentieth-century poet,
and thus his rich heritage has been brought to bear on our
times. No one who knows modern poetry will say that Hopkins
has remained "Time's eunuch"; his prayer has been answered,
for apparently some rain has come to his poetic roots.

Postscript

There is no need now to establish Hopkins as a major poet. He has been proclaimed so, far and wide. More and more readers are discovering him and finding proofs for statements of his genius. Literary historians have noted his influence on contemporary writers, some even committing themselves to broad general statements of his stature. Mr. F. R. Leavis is an example. He wrote of Hopkins: "He is likely to prove, for our time and the future, the only influential poet of the Victorian age, and he seems to me the greatest."[1]

However, there is need to show what unique characteristics make Hopkins' art peculiarly his. There is need to answer that question that Hopkins himself asked of all artistic creation: What unmistakable mark or stamp does it bear? It may be argued that this question has already been settled by critics who have studied Hopkins' poetic diction and sprung rhythm because these form the "scape" of his poetry. While it cannot be denied that these are integral elements in Hopkins' art, to accept them as all would be to accept the formal principles of poetry as the whole significance of the poetic art. But what about the first question that any reader asks: What does it say?

When this question is answered regarding Hopkins poetry, it usually amounts to a broad classification, such as religious, Christian, or Catholic. To settle for such an explanation of the meaning of Hopkins' poetry is to be satisfied with crude historicity. This reading of his poetry has attempted to indicate how unacceptable an answer this is. I have tried to show that most of Hopkins' poetry is strikingly consonant with the spirituality of St. Ignatius as embodied in his Spiritual Exercises. I have had an obvious edge in that Hopkins himself was a member of the Society of Jesus, and thus the Spiritual Exercises became the spiritual director of his whole life. The prob-

ability was that they did influence his art. I have attempted
to indicate the extraordinarily close kinship between Exercises
and Hopkins' body poetic, which makes the influence a defined
fact.

One of the things that bothers many a modern critic of
Hopkins is that the Jesuit priest overrode the brilliant poet.
They ask why and answer, whatever it was, it frustrated the
poet. The answer why is Ignatius who wrote in the Constitutions of his order regarding all pursuits and endeavors that
members of the Society "must diligently observe, esteeming it
of great importance and of the highest moment in the sight
of our Creator and Lord, how much it helps and contributes to
progress in spiritual life, to abhor wholly and not in part
what the world loves and embraces, and to accept and desire
with their whole strength whatsoever Christ our Lord loved
and embraced. For as worldly men, who follow the things of
the world, love and with great diligence seek honours, reputa-
tion and the credit of a great name upon earth, as the world
teaches them, so those who are advancing in spirit and seriously
follow Christ our Lord, love and earnestly desire things which
are altogether the contrary. . . ."[2] More often than not, Hopkins judged that his poetry did not advance his spirituality,
and when he did write, his vocation determined him all the
more to express his first purpose in life.

Though his early poetry is religiously inclined, the poetry
of his Jesuit years is primarily religious. Some critics argue that
this mature verse is not religious, but only pious and reflective.
They base their argument on their observation that the senses
dominate in these poems, rather than any spiritual significance.
This is to ignore or not fully accept Hopkins' strongly Ignatian
attitude that all creatures were made for man's use to lead him
back to his Creator. The natural beauty of all things is significantly enhanced by their supernatural significance. This sacramental view of the universe really meant something to Hopkins,
and he expressed it so often in his mature poetry, that it must
be reckoned as one of his major themes. The sensuous imagery
of these poems in no way contends with this sacramental view.
In fact, to portray creation as anything else but good and

beautiful would be to say that God's manifestation of Himself was defective, low, and ugly. The very basis of a sacramental view of all existence is its God-given and God-sustained splendor. Hopkins always presented nature as glorious "news of God"; when nature is spoiled, it is, he wrote, because it has been "manhandled." Those readers who see only the reflection of natural beauty in Hopkins' poetry and refuse to see that dimension of meaning beyond the natural, what Hopkins called "immortal beauty," miss, it seems to me, the real spiritual profundity of his art. This is unfortunate, for Hopkins is one of the few poets in the English language who could imaginatively express the imminent presence of God in all things. Perhaps he is undone by the modern mind and its inability to understand Christian contempt of the world as anything else than a complete rejection of all earthly existence.

It can be admitted that the Jesuit priest frustrated certain more secular tendencies in Hopkins' poetry, but why stop here? Did not the Jesuit priest enhance the spiritual scope, depth, and significance of the mature poetry? Certainly there is nothing wrongheaded in thinking that when Hopkins chose to express through his superb poetic gifts the feelings and thoughts to which he had solemnly dedicated his life, the poet and the priest collaborated most successfully. Those readers who constantly insist otherwise are often those who read parts of poems and praise their beauty, such as the octave of the "The Windhover" sonnet. Somehow those passages of spiritual insight in the poems get less attention, even though these are often the high points poetically. The critical fact is that Hopkins was seldom just poet; the priest in him converted the artist.

Hopkins expressed to an imposing extent both the spirit and ideals of St. Ignatius. Since he chose to live his life according to the spirit and disciplines of St. Ignatius' Company, and since, as I have tried to indicate, so much of his poetry can be so fully and fruitfully read in the light of the Spiritual Exercises, there is no question of the makeup of Hopkins' mind nor the ground of his poetic art. Both must be specified as Ignatian. To assert this is to assert greater compatibility between priest

and poet than many contemporary scholars admit. It is also
to assert that the basis of Hopkins' importance as a poet does
not lie primarily, as modern scholars have often said, in those
poems when the poet seemed to triumph over the priest, but
rather in his grand attempts to fuse the poet and priest, the result
of which produced the finest religious verse since the seventeenth century.

Against the rejoinder that the "terrible" sonnets are most
certainly examples of priest and poet at odds, must be put the
whole concept of spiritual disconsolation, which has a long
history in the Christian spiritual tradition. And it is nowhere
more central in the tradition than in the Spiritual Exercises of
St. Ignatius. From his own religious experience Ignatius saw the
necessity of knowing when he was being moved by God and
when he was not, and thus he drew up a set of rules for the
discernment of spirits. When the members of his Company
experienced periods of depression and defeat, the action of the
Holy Spirit not always being sweet, they had through their
founder a practical strategy for the management of their
spiritual lives. One noted commentator wrote of this section
of the Exercises, "It is the heart of Ignatian spirituality; the
inner source of every apostolic life since it is an absolute necessity to 'discern' the action of the Holy Spirit from that of the
Devil."[3]

I have tried to point out that whatever were the sources of
Hopkins' disconsolation in Ireland, the poems he wrote expressing his discomfiture exhibit Hopkins' attempt to discern the
spirit of God in his suffering and to accept his plight, difficult
as it was, in order to advance his spiritual life. Nothing could be
more Ignatian. This would suggest that that element in the
poems of probing the spirit of God ought to be equally stressed
with the striking depictions in them of depression and suffering.
Moreover, a great deal of elucidation might be had in the
Patristic and Scholastic traditions to go along with what has been
gleaned from modern psychology. The result should be a fuller
and richer reading of those poems which depict Hopkins'
"winter world."

Not only is the vision to which Hopkins gave expression

essentially Ignatian, but, in my opinion, some of his poetic forms seem to have derived from the structure of the Ignatian meditation. Controversial as it is, there are reasons for saying this. The structure of methodical meditation has often been observed as paralleling, in general, the poetic act. This is especially true in the writing of religious poetry that is primarily reflective and meditative. When the movement and manner of some of Hopkins' poems are set beside the Ignatian methods of prayer, their comparison would argue to considerable influence. His poems are not Ignatian meditations poetized, but they are often poetic approximations of some of the dispositions and methods of Ignatian prayer. It surely should not be surprising that this be so in the case of one who was both priest and poet.

Priest and poet has been said of Hopkins before, but it has been asserted largely on biographical lines. The question posed is: How are the poet and priest related in the art? I have gone to great lengths to demonstrate that the answer to this question is by means of a very tautly applied Ignatian religious discipline. To some, my endeavor will seem a long way to go for what they consider just a nuance, but those who discriminate various spiritual traditions of religious poetry will consider this delineation much more than a detail. For these, a very important religious poet will have been placed within his proper historico-critical context: Ignatian Christianity and meditative genre. Moreover, as a Jesuit poet, Gerard Hopkins celebrated in his writing—more beautifully than any other poet in the Society—that basic wisdom and vision that Ignatius gave to his Company: *"Ad Majorem Dei Gloriam."* This must be added to sprung rhythm, poetic diction, and other artistic considerations to make an adequate definition of Hopkins' poetic art, to more fully appreciate it, to truly give it honor.

For the agnostic critic or reader, the decidedly Ignatian intellectual element in Hopkins' fourteen hundred lines is a weakness because such a point of view assumes that Christian beliefs and principles are so many emotional oddities having small claim on the mind. One cannot but wonder at the imposing task of proving that those poets writing from passionate doubt have produced a body of ideas and attitudes that are clearly more valuable than those that have emanated from the fullest and richest Christian predispositions.

Nevertheless, to such readers this attempt to explicate the philosophic thought of Hopkins will seem an aside. To these, my appeal must be historic. It is, however, to the credit of such readers that, despite the Christian content of Hopkins' art, they have tried to read him on his own ground, to discover his genuine poetic self, difficult as it is to divorce form and matter. Many of these lay claim to at least part of the poet. No doubt, it is for the reader disposed "to apprehend/The point of intersection of the timeless/With time," that Hopkins' intricate harmonies are powerful and compelling testaments of man's sublimest aspiration: to know Divinity.

Notes

INTRODUCTION

1. See Alexander Brou, *Les Exercises Spirituels de Saint Ignace de Loyola. Histoire et Psychologie* (2nd ed., Paris: P. Tequi, 1922). See also James Broderick, *The Origin of the Jesuits,* (London: Longmans, Green, 1940); and *The Progress of the Jesuits* (1556-79), (London: Longmans, Green, 1947).

2. Louis Martz, *The Poetry of Meditation* (New Haven: Yale University Press, 1954).

3. *Ibid.*, p. 4.

4. Cf. bibliography

I

1. G. F. Lahey, S.J., *Gerard Manley Hopkins* (London: Oxford Univ. Press, 1930), pp. 33-34. Hereafter cited as *Life.*

2. *Ibid.*, p. 35.

3. *Further Letters of Gerard Manley Hopkins including his Correspondence with Coventry Patmore,* ed. C. C. Abbott (London: Oxford Univ. Press, 1938), p. 17. Hereafter cited as *Further Letters.*

4. *Ibid.*

5. *The Letters of Gerard Manley Hopkins to Robert Bridges,* ed. C. C. Abbott (London: Oxford Univ. Press, 1935), pp. 5-6. Hereafter cited as *Letters to Bridges.*

6. *Further Letters,* p. 19.

7. *Ibid.*, p. 20.

8. *Letters to Bridges,* p. 22.

9. *Further Letters,* p. 261.

10. Hopkins was just over five feet.

11. More than once he recorded special lights he had received that he considered as of divine origin.

12. Hugo Rahner, S.J., *The Spirituality of St. Ignatius Loyola* (Westminster, Maryland: The Newman Press, 1953), p. xi.

13. John Pick, *Gerard Manley Hopkins* (London: Oxford University Press, 1942), pp. 25-26.

II

1. The latest unscrambling is by Alan Heuser in his *The Shaping Vision of Gerard Manley Hopkins* (Oxford, 1958). Father Christopher Devlin, S.J., has done the major job of finding the key parts in a series he wrote for *The Month*. Cf. the bibliography.

2. G. M. Hopkins, *The Note-Books and Papers of Gerard Manley Hopkins,* ed. Humphry House (London: Oxford University Press, 1937), p. 250. Hereafter cited as *Note-Books*.

3. *Ibid.,* p. 108.

4. *Ibid.,* p. 149.

5. *Ibid.,* p. 310.

6. *Ibid.,* p. 98.

7. *Ibid.,* p. 351.

8. *Ibid.,* p. 344.

9. W. A. M. Peters, S.J., *Gerard Manley Hopkins* (London: Oxford University Press, 1948), pp. 14-15.

10. G. M. Hopkins, *The Letters of Gerard Manley Hopkins to Robert Bridges,* ed. C. C. Abbott (London: Oxford University Press, 1935), p. 66. Hereafter cited as *Letters to Bridges*.

11. G. M. Hopkins, *Further Letters of Gerard Manley Hopkins including his Correspondence with Coventry Patmore,* ed. C. C. Abbott (London: Oxford University Press, 1938), p. 84.

12. He beautifully commended Scotus in a poem as, "Of reality the rarest-veined unraveller; a not/Rivalled insight. . . ."

13. *Note-Books,* p. 161.

14. *Note-Books,* p. XXXIII

15. *Letters to Bridges,* p. 150.

16. Peters, p. 23.

17. *Note-Books,* pp. 309-310.

18. S. J. Curtis, *A Short History of Western Philosophy in the Middle Ages* (Westminster, Md.: The Newman Press, 1950), p. 227.

19. They would argue that there is no analogy of being provided for.

20. *Note-Books,* p. 316.

21. The last exercise in The Spiritual Exercises.

176   GERARD MANLEY HOPKINS: *A Study of His Ignatian Spirit*

22. *Note-Books*, p. 342.

23. *Ibid.*, p. 134.

24. *Ibid.*, p. 205.

25. I would refer the reader to Father Christopher Devlin's excellent analysis of Hopkins' theological notions in his edition of Hopkins' spiritual writings. Cf. bibliography.

26. Curtis, p. 226.

27. *Note-Books*, p. 317.

28. *Ibid.*, p. 326.

29. *Ibid.*, p. 328.

30. *Ibid.*, p. 322.

31. *Ibid.*, p. 323.

32. *Ibid.*, p. 328.

33. *Ibid.*

34. *Ibid.*, p. 321.

35. *Ibid.*

36. *Ibid.*, p. 318.

37. *Ibid.*, p. 323.

38. *Ibid.*, p. 324.

39. *Ibid.*, p. 325.

40. *Ibid.*, p. 333.

41. *Ibid.*, p. 332.

42. *Ibid.*, pp. 328-329.

43. *Ibid.*, p. 332.

44. *Ibid.*, p. 337.

45. *Ibid.*

46. *Ibid.*, p. 338.

47. *Ibid.*

48. *Ibid.*

49. *Ibid.*, p. 332.

50. Hugo Rahner, *The Spirituality of St. Ignatius Loyola* (Westminster, Maryland: The Newman Press, 1935), p. 36.

51. Unpublished *ms.* (Campion Hall, Oxford), R. Commentary on the Spiritual Exercises. (This has been recently published in a new elition of H's papers.)

52. *Note-Books*, p. 343.

III

1. *The Correspondence of Gerard Manley Hopkins and Richard Watson Dixon*, ed. C. C. Abbott (London: Oxford

University Press, 1935), p. 14.

2. *Note-Books and Papers of Gerard Manley Hopkins,* ed. H. House (London: Oxford University Press, 1937), p. 210. Hereafter cited as *Note-Books.*

3. His sister Grace burned the religious Journal, but D. A. Bischoff, S.J., has pointed out that she did not know what she burned since she did not even read a line (beyond Gerard's injunction not to read). The question of a religious Journal remains at best a conjecture.

4. *Note-Books,* p. 121.

5. *Ibid.,* p. 135.

6. *Ibid.*

7. It can be argued that Hopkins was here referring to his conversion to Catholicism, though there is no evidence to support this and the arguments from probability are weak. It also can be argued that he was referring to his retreat at the Jesuit Novitiate. Whether Father Henry Coleridge used the Spiritual Exercises in giving this retreat, I do not know. I have taken what I think is the most probable explanation, that Hopkins was referring to that first intense spiritual experience that he had as a Jesuit novice, the Spiritual Exercises, from which came that supreme election of giving all back to God. Whatever view is taken, the important fact is that there is a notable harmony between the spirit of Ignatius as Hopkins perceived it and the spirit of the poem, especially in the intensely personal first part.

8. F. R. Leavis, *New Bearings in English Poetry* (London: Chatto and Windus, 1950), pp. 175-176.

9. *Ibid.,* p. 176.

10. *The Letters of Gerard Manley Hopkins to Robert Bridges,* ed. C. C. Abbott (London: Oxford University Press, 1935), p. 47.

11. Unpublished *ms.* (Campion Hall, Oxford), R. Commentary on the Spiritual Exercises.

12. In his comment Hopkins called "quickening" grace the grace of novices, "corrective" the elective grace, "elevating" the grace of the Holy Spirit through the Eucharist. The *Commentary* is a later, more detailed version of the allusions in his ode.

13. *Note-Books,* p. 337.

14. Ignatius Loyola, *The Spiritual Exercises* (Westminster, Md.: The Newman Bookshop, 1943), p. 24. Hereafter cited as *S. E.*

15. *Ibid.,* p. 25.

16. Host most certainly means Eucharist here, thus "elevating" grace. The important point is the afflictive stress of God's grace and the elective instress of that grace by man.

17. *Note-Books,* p. 333.

18. *Ibid.,* p. 325.

19. Recall Scotus' first act of knowing which is visionary insight, a look into the divine mind, as it were.

20. *S. E.,* p. 12.

21. *Note-Books,* p. 330.

22. *Ibid.,* p. 332.

23. I have relied generally upon the account in *Immortal Diamond: Studies in Gerard Manley Hopkins,* edited by Norman Weyand, S.J. (Sheed and Ward, 1949).

24. *Immortal Diamond: Studies in Gerard Manley Hopkins,* ed. N. Weyand, S.J. (New York: Sheed and Ward, 1949), p. 360.

25. *Ibid.,* p. 368.

26. *Ibid.,* p. 374.

27. *Ibid.,* p. 368.

28. Unpublished *ms.* (Campion Hall, Oxford), R. Commentary on Spiritual Exercises.

29. Hopkins telescoped in this stanza much of Mariology: "Feast of the one woman without stain," Feast of the Immaculate Conception (the day after the wreck—"the feast that followed the night"); and "For so conceived . . . Word . . .," Feast of the Incarnation. Cf. Stanzas 6 and 7 in Part I for corelation.

30. *Note-Books,* p. 332.

31. *Poems of Gerard Manley Hopkins,* ed. W. H. Gardner (London: Oxford University Press, 1948), p. 95.

32. *Ibid.,* p. 112.

IV

1. I am not suggesting that these poems so arranged amount to a poetic version of the Spiritual Exercises though an impressive number of them—some of the best—amount to a poetic version of an Ignatian meditation.

2. I do not see how it can be denied that they were fulfilled. He was true to his vocation throughout his life, and, in his chosen way, wrote poetry which has brought him to the front

ranks of British poets. Those who think he sacrificed the poet, at times with great hardships, are faced with the fact that he wanted it this way. Unlike the negation of evil, the denial of something supremely good as an act of love is difficult to understand. It is a rare quality of love.

3. *Poems of Gerard Manley Hopkins,* ed. W. H. Gardner (London: Oxford University Press, 1948), p. 40. Hereafter cited as *Poems.*

4. *Ibid.,* p. 43.

5. Ignatius Loyola, *The Spiritual Exercises* (Westminster, Md.: The Newman Bookshop, 1943), p. 3. Hereafter cited as *S. E.*

6. *Poems,* pp. 46-47.

7. *Ibid.,* p. 72.

8. *Ibid.,* pp. 72-73.

9. *Ibid.,* p. 113.

10. *Ibid.,* p. 65.

11. *Ibid.,* p. 96.

12. *Ibid.,* p. 74.

13. *Ibid.,* pp. 96-98.

14. *Ibid.,* p. 167.

15. *Ibid.*

16. *Ibid.,* p. 76.

17. Comment on Ignatian meditation and artistic creativity is made in the section on Hopkins and the Meditative Tradition. My interest throughout this section is thematic.

18. *Poems,* p. 75.

19. *Ibid.,* p. 173.

20. *Ibid.,* p. 94.

21. *Ibid.,* p. 71.

22. *Ibid.,* p. 112.

23. *Ibid.,* p. 59.

24. *Ibid.,* p. 170.

25. *Ibid.,* pp. 156-157.

26. *Ibid.,* p. 90.

27. *Ibid.,* p. 110.

28. *S. E.,* pp. 24-25.

29. *Poems,* pp. 86-87.

30. *Ibid.,* p. 58.

31. Recall (Hopkins through Scotus): Christ's human nature is the perfect finite image of the Divine Essence.

32. *Poems,* p. 170.

33. *Ibid.,* p. 166.

34. Recall Hopkins' notion of *pitch* as a pre-existing determination of man towards his divine destiny, God. This is what he called human personality.

35. *S. E.,* p. 34.

36. *Poems,* p. 105.

37. *Ibid.,* p. 80.

38. *Ibid.,* p. 88.

39. *Ibid.,* p. 95.

40. Here Hopkins, following Scotus' theology of the Incarnation, amplified Ignatius by saying that Christ was predestined before all other creatures, which destiny encompassed His Great Sacrifice. Mary was a part of that destiny.

41. *Poems,* pp. 100-101.

42. He described his summons to Dublin as "inconvenient and painful," likened it to the summons of Joseph and Mary to Bethlehem, declared, ". . . I am bound in justice, and paid."

43. *Poems,* pp. 102-103.

44. *Ibid.,* p. 82.

45. *Ibid.,* p. 104.

46. This is an excellent example of what I called that evocative soul-leap through and beyond nature to the Eternal and Divine in Hopkins' verse.

47. *Poems,* p. 105.

48. The MSS reveal that this dedication was added some time after the poem was composed. However, it makes little difference for the poet's intention is clearly revealed in the poem.

49. The Election is really the climax of the meditation on the Kingdom of Christ which marks the turn in the Exercises from divine justice in the First Week to divine mercy in the Second. The context of this poem is this meditation as it is for the Election.

50. *Poems,* p. 73.

51. Tradition has it that when Ignatius sent St. Francis Xavier to India, he said, *"Ite,* incendite omnia," "go and set everything on fire." At the time of his conversion, Ignatius described his disposition as "a magnanimous heart, inflamed by God."

52. Hugo Rahner, S.J., *The Spirituality of St. Ignatius Loyola,*

trans. by Francis John Smith, S.J. (Maryland: The Newman Press, 1953), p. 35.

53. Pere Paul Dudon, S.J., *St. Ignatius of Loyola,* trans. by William Young, S.J. (Milwaukee: The Bruce Publishing Co., 1949), p. 56.

54. It is possible that there are two figures here (plowing and hot ashes). The first suggests the splendor of spirit hidden beneath accidentals dutifully performed; the second reinforces the first using the analogy of cooling ashes in a banked fire.

55. *Poems,* p. 33.

56. *Ibid.,* pp. 103-104.

57. W. H. Gardner, *Gerard Manley Hopkins, 1844-1889* (New Haven: Yale University Press, 1949), vol. II, p. 319.

58. *Poems,* pp. 112-113.

59. *Ibid.,* p. 28.

60. *Ibid.,* p. 62.

61. *Note-Books and Papers of Gerard Manley Hopkins,* ed. H. House (London: Oxford University Press, 1937), p. 128.

62. *Poems,* pp. 38-39.

63. It is both the thematic as well as poetic climax in "The Wreck" epitomized in the lines, ". . . Our passion-plunged giant risen,/The Christ of the Father compassionate, fetched in the storm of his strides."

64. *Poems,* p. 28.

65. *Ibid.,* p. 35.

66. *Ibid.,* p. 45.

67. *Ibid.,* p. 112

68. *Ibid.,* p. 76.

69. *Ibid.,* p. 37.

70. *Ibid.,* pp. 74-75.

V

1. *Note-Books and Papers of Gerard Manley Hopkins,* ed. H. House (London: Oxford University Press, 1937), p. 8. Hereafter cited as *Note-Books.*

2. *Ibid.,* p. 9.

3. *Ibid.,* p. 10.

4. *Ibid.,* p. 32.

5. *Poems of Gerard Manley Hopkins,* ed. W. H. Gardner

(London: Oxford University Press, 1948), pp. 24-25. Hereafter cited as *Poems.*

6. *Ibid.,* p. 33.

7. *Note-Books,* p. 53.

8. *Ibid.,* p. 210.

9. *The Correspondence of Gerard Manley Hopkins and Richard Watson Dixon,* ed. C. C. Abbott (London: Oxford University Press, 1935), p. 27.

10. *Ibid.,* p. 15.

11. *Ibid.,* p. 28.

12. *The Correspondence of Gerard Manley Hopkins to Robert Bridges,* ed. C. C. Abbott (London: Oxford University Press, 1935), p. 66.

13. *Poems,* pp. xix-xx.

14. *Correspondence to Dixon,* p. 80.

15. *Ibid.,* p. 88.

16. *Ibid.,* p. 93.

17. *Ibid.,* pp. 93-94.

18. *Ibid.,* pp. 95-96.

19. *Ibid.,* p. 96.

20. *Correspondence to Bridges,* p. 190.

21. *Ibid.,* p. 216.

22. *Further Letters of Gerard Manley Hopkins including his Correspondence with Coventry Patmore,* ed. C. C. Abbott (London: Oxford University Press, 1938), pp. 109-110.

23. *Correspondence to Bridges,* p. 221.

24. *Poems,* p. 109.

25. *Correspondence to Bridges,* pp. 218-219.

26. *Correspondence to Dixon,* p. 139.

27. *Ibid.,* p. 150.

28. *Correspondence to Bridges,* p. 270.

29. G. F. Lahey, S.J., *Gerard Manley Hopkins* (London: Oxford University Press, 1938), pp. 140-144 *passim.*

30. *Ibid.,* p. 142.

31. *Ibid.,* p. 143.

32. *Poems,* p. xx.

33. *Further Letters,* pp. 84-85.

34. Hopkins described this state in his *Commentary:* "So that while we strive, though we commit faults, we are not luke-warm; when we give up struggling and let ourselves drift, then tepidity begins."

35. Bk. II, Ch. 10.

36. *Modern American and Modern British Poetry*, ed. Louis Untermeyer and others (New York: Harcourt Brace, 1955), p. 454.

37. Ignatius was very reserved as to mystical states, did not consider them as unquestioned signs of perfection. Cf. P. Pourrat, *Christian Spirituality*, vol. III.

38. This includes Calvinistic Protestantism in Hopkins' case.

39. *Poems*, p. xxi.

40. Hugo Rahner, S.J., *The Spirituality of St. Ignatius Loyola* (Maryland: The Newman Press, 1953), pp. 24-25.

41. However the Exercises are not regarded as a complete manual of asceticism leading to mysticism. Ignatius' goal was to give God more missioners; the mystics he left to God.

42. Ignatius Loyola, *The Spiritual Exercises* (Westminster, Md.: The Newman Bookshop, 1943), p. 111. Hereafter cited as S. E.

43. *Ibid.*, p. 107.

44. Thomas a Kempis, *The Following of Christ*, ed. Rev. J. M. Lelen, Ph.D. (New York: Catholic Book Publishing Co., 1941), p. 136. Hereafter cited as Kempis.

45. *Ibid.*, p. 138.

46. The final renunciation seems to have taken place during a retreat at Beaumont, 1883, a decision clearly against his desires which the last years in Dublin heavily underscore.

47. *Poems*, p. 36.

48. Father Devlin thinks this un-Catholic; however, there is a very considerable body of Catholic writing to support this notion of Christian perfection. It does go against the grain of modern Catholicism though.

49. *Ibid.*, p. 56.

50. *S. E.*, p. 106.

51. *Ibid.*, pp. 108-109.

52. *Ibid.*, p. 109.

53. *Poems*, pp. 109-110.

54. Kempis, p. 159.

55. *Ibid.*, p. 91.

56. *Ibid.*, p. 160.

57. *Ibid.*, p. 238.

58. *Poems*, pp. 106-107.

59. Kempis, p. 274.

60. *Ibid.,* pp. 39-40.
61. *Ibid.,* pp. 139-140
62. *Ibid.,* p. 280.
63. *S. E.,* p. 108.
64. Kempis, pp. 284-285.
65. *Ibid.,* pp. 140-141.
66. *Ibid.,* pp. 155-156.
67. *Ibid.,* p. 349.
68. *Ibid.,* p. 140.
69. *S. E.,* p. 108.
70. *Ibid.*
71. *Poems,* p. 106.
72. Kempis, p. 276.
73. *Ibid.,* p. 352.
74. *Poems,* p. 113.
75. Kempis, pp. 276-277.
76. *S. E.,* pp. 111-112.
77. Kempis, p. 275.
78. *Ibid.,* p. 233.
79. *Ibid.,* p. 235.
80. *Poems,* p. 106.
81. Kempis, p. 352.
82. *Ibid.,* pp. 358-359.
83. *Ibid.,* p. 230.
84. *Ibid.,* p. 275.
85. *Ibid.,* p. 143.
86. *Poems,* p. 110.
87. Kempis, pp. 138-139.
88. *S. E.,* pp. 111-112.
89. *Poems,* pp. 110-111.
90. *Ibid.,* p. 112.
91. *S. E.,* p. 125.
92. The same seems to be true in his spiritual life. During a retreat at Beaumont (1883) he was advised to stop the consideration of his own sins. This was probably a frequent counsel in his case.
93. The retreat of January, 1889, for example, brought him to the peaceful assurances of Christ in the Second Week despite a most ruthless self-examination, as his private notes make clear.
94. *Note-Books,* pp. 416-417.

95. *Ibid.,* p. 417.

96. *Ibid.,* p. 416.

97. *S. E.,* p. 107.

VI

1. Etienne Gilson, *The Philosophy of St. Bonaventure,* trans. Illtyd Trethowan and F. J. Sheed (New York, Sheed and Ward, 1938), p. 224.

2. *Poems of Gerard Manley Hopkins,* ed. W. H. Gardner (London: Oxford University Press, 1948), p. 104.

3. *Ibid.,* p. 74.

4. *Ibid.,* p. 73.

5. Which may be the reason that Father M. C. D'Arcy, the distinguished Jesuit scholar, considers the ending of this sonnet to be artistically weak.

6. *Poems of Gerard Manley Hopkins,* ed. W. H. Gardner (London: Oxford University Press, 1948), p. 70.

7. *Ibid.,* p. 74.

8. Recall Hopkins' notion that all degrees of natural perfection were summed up in Christ.

9. Thus proving how wrongheaded those readers are who dissociate the sensuous from the religious aspects of Hopkins' poetry. To do so is to shatter religion, art, and any genuine love.

10. *Poems of Gerard Manley Hopkins,* ed. W. H. Gardner (London: Oxford University Press, 1948), pp. 55-67.

11. *Ibid.,* p. 95.

12. *Ibid.,* p. 86.

13. *Ibid.,* p. 111.

14. *Ibid.,* p. 50.

15. *Ibid.,* pp. 81-82.

16. *Ibid.,* pp. 99-103.

17. Recall Hopkins' notion that Mary was one of the gifts of Christ's great sacrifice; through the Eucharist, she still bears Christ to man: "New Bethlems, and he born/There, evening, noon, and morn—"

18. Louis Martz, *The Poetry of Meditation* (New Haven: Yale University Press, 1954), p. 324.

19. *Ibid.*

20. *Ibid.*

POSTSCRIPT

1. F. R. Leavis, *New Bearings in English Poetry* (London: Chatto and Windus, 1950), p. 193.

2. *Summary of the Constitutions* (Roehampton: Manresa Press, 1926), p. 6.

3. Ignacio Iparraguirre, S.J., *A Key to the Study of the Spiritual Exercises,* trans. by J. Chianese, S.J., (Calcutta: Hibernian Press), p. 99.

Selected Bibliography

A. HOPKINS' WORKS

Poems of Gerard Manley Hopkins, third edition, the first edition with preface and notes by Robert Bridges enlarged and edited with notes and a biographical introduction by W. H. Gardner, third impression. London, 1950.

Poems and Prose of Gerard Manley Hopkins, selected with an introduction and notes by W. H. Gardner, Penguin Poets D 15. London, 1953.

The Letters of Gerard Manley Hopkins to Robert Bridges, edited with notes and an introduction by Claude Colleer Abbott. London, 1935, 1955.

The Correspondence of Gerard Manley Hopkins and Richard Watson Dixon, edited with notes and an introduction by Claude Colleer Abbott. London, 1935, 1955.

Further Letters of Gerard Manley Hopkins Including His Correspondence with Coventry Patmore, edited with notes and an introduction by Claude Colleer Abbott, second edition revised and enlarged. London, 1956.

The Note-Books and Papers of Gerard Manley Hopkins, edited with notes and an introduction by Humphry House. London, 1937. To be published by the Oxford University Press in 1959, in two volumes: *Journals and Papers,* edited by Humphry House and completed by Graham Storey, and *Sermons and Devotional Writings,* edited by Christopher Devlin, S.J. London, 1959. The two volumes together constitute the second edition revised and enlarged of *The Note-Books and Papers of Gerard Manley Hopkins,* edited by Humphry House, 1937.

B. SECONDARY WORKS

AMBRUZZI, ALOYSIUS, S.J. *The Spiritual Exercises of Saint Ignatius.* London: Coldwell Ltd., 1931.

BISCHOFF, D. ANTHONY, S.J. "The Manuscripts of Gerard Manley Hopkins," *Thought,* XXV (1951), 551-80.

BREMOND, HENRI. *A Literary History of Religious Thought in France,* trans. K. L. Montgomery. 3 Vols. London: S.P.C.K., 1928-36.

BRODERICK, JAMES, S.J. *The Origin of the Jesuits.* New York: Longmans, Green and Company, 1940.

BROU, ALEXANDRE, S.J. *Ignatian Methods of Prayer,* trans. by William J. Young, S.J. Milwaukee: The Bruce Publishing Company, 1949.

CALVERAS, JOSE P., S.J. *The Harvest-Field of the Spiritual Exercises of Saint Ignatius,* trans. by J. H. Gense, S.J. Bombay: St. Xavier's College, 1949.

CHARMOT, FRANCOIS. "Discernment des esprits et direction," *Christus,* No. 5 (January, 1955), 29-38.

CHARNEY, MAURICE. "A Bibliographical Study of Hopkins Criticism, 1918-1949," *Thought,* XXV (1950), 297-326.

COOGAN, MARJORIE D. "Inscape and Instress: Further Analogies with Scotus," *PMLA,* LXV (March, 1950), 66-75.

CURTIS, S. J. *A Short History of Western Philosophy in the Middle Ages.* Westminster, Maryland: The Newman Press, 1950.

DANIELOU, JEAN, S.J. "The Ignatian Vision of the Universe and of Man," *Crosscurrents,* IV (Fall, 1954), 357.

D'ARCY, MARTIN C., S.J. "Gerard Manley Hopkins," *Month,* CLXXXI (1945), 67-9.

————, "Gerard Manley Hopkins," *Great Catholics,* ed. Claude Williamson. New York: Macmillan Company, 1939.

DERKS, GEORGES, S.J. "The Psychology of the Exercises," *Woodstock Letters,* 76, (1949), 297-319.

DEVLIN, CHRISTOPHER, S.J. "An Essay on Scotus," *Month,* CLXXXII (1946), 456-66.

————, "Hopkins and Duns Scotus," *New Verse,* No. 14 (April, 1935), 12-17.

————, "The Ignatian Inspiration of Gerard Hopkins," *Blackfriars,* XVI (1935), 887-900.

————, "The Image and the Word," *Month,* N. S., III (1950), 114-27, 191-202.

————, Letter to the Editor, *Month,* N. S., IV (1950), 213-15.

————, *The Psychology of Duns Scotus.* London Aquinas Society. Oxford, 1950.

————, "Time's Eunuch," *Month*, N. S., I (1949), 303-12.

DONNELLY, PHILIP J., S.J. "Dogma and the Spiritual Exercises," *Woodstock Letters*, (May, 1954), 131-157.

DUDON, PAUL, S.J. *St. Ignatius of Loyola*, trans. by William J. Young, S.J. Milwaukee: The Bruce Publishing Company, 1949.

EMPSON, WILLIAM. *Seven Types of Ambiguity*. London: Chatto and Windus, 1930.

GANSS, GEORGE E., S.J. "St. Ignatius' Constitution and the Spirit of the Ratio," *Jesuit Educational Quarterly*, XVII, No. 2 (October, 1954), 69-82.

GARDNER, W. H. *Gerard Manley Hopkins*, Vol. I. London: Martin Secker and Warburg, 1948.

————, *Gerard Manley Hopkins*. Vol. II. New Haven: Yale University Press, 1949.

————, "The Wreck of the Deutschland," *Essays and Studies*, XXI (1936), 124-152.

GILSON, ETIENNE. *The Mystical Theology of Saint Bernard*, trans. by A. H. C. Downes. New York: Sheed and Ward, 1938.

————, *The Philosophy of St. Bonaventure*, trans. by Illtyd Trethowan and F. J. Sheed. New York: Sheed and Ward, 1938.

GONZALEZ DE CAMARA, LUIS. *St. Ignatius' Own Story*, trans. by William J. Young, S.J. Chicago: Henry Regnery Co., 1956.

HEUSER, ALAN. *The Shaping Vision of Gerard Manley Hopkins*. London: Oxford University Press, 1958.

Imitation of Christ, The. From the First Edition of an English Translation Made c. 1530 by Richard Whitford. Ed. by Edward J. Klein. New York: Harper, 1941.

IPARRAGUIRRE, IGNACIO, S.J. *A Key to the Study of the Spiritual Exercises*, trans. by J. Chianese, S.J. Calcutta: Hibernian Press, 1955.

————, "Introduction to the Spiritual Exercises," *Woodstock Letters* (July, 1955), 211-260.

KELLEY, BERNARD. *The Mind and Poetry of Gerard Manley Hopkins*. London: Pepler and Sewell, 1935.

KELLEY, HEINRICH, S.J. "Jesuit Obedience," *Woodstock Letters*, 76, (1949), 37-46.

THE KENYON CRITICS. *Gerard Manley Hopkins*. Norfolk, Connecticut: New Directions Books, 1945.

LAHEY, G. F., S.J. *Gerard Manley Hopkins*. London: Oxford
  University Press, 1938.

——————, "Gerard Manley Hopkins," *The Commonweal*, XVIII
  (October, 1933), 581-584.

LEAVIS, F. R. *New Bearings in English Poetry*. London: Chatto
  and Windus, 1950.

LITTLE, ARTHUR, S.J. "The Problem of 'The Contemplation
  for Obtaining Love,'" *The Irish Ecclesiastical Record*,
  Fifth Series: LXXIII (January, 1950), 13-25.

LOARTE, GASPAR. *The Exercise of a Christian Life*, [trans. by
  Stephen Brinkley. Rheins?], 1584.

LOYOLA, IGNATIUS. *The Spiritual Exercises*. Preface signed by
  John Morris, S.J. Westminster, Maryland: The Newman
  Bookshop, 1943.

MARITAIN, JACQUES. *Creative Intuition in Art and Poetry*. London: Pantheon Books, 1954.

MARTZ, LOUIS. *The Poetry of Meditation*. New Haven: Yale
  University Press, 1954.

MAS, JAMES NONELL. *Los Ejercicios Espirituales de N. P. S.
  Ignacio*. Manresa: 1896.

MATT, LEONARD VON, and HUGO RAHNER, S.J. *St. Ignatius of
  Loyola*, trans. by John Murray, S.J. Chicago: Henry Regnery
  Co., 1956.

O'CONOR, J. F. X., S.J., ed. *The Autobiography of St. Ignatius*.
  New York: Benziger Brothers, 1900.

PETERS, S. A. M., S.J. *Gerard Manley Hopkins*. London: Oxford
  University Press, 1948.

PHARE, E. E. *The Poetry of Gerard Manley Hopkins*. Cambridge:
  Cambridge University Press, 1933.

PICK, JOHN. *Gerard Manley Hopkins: Priest and Poet*. London:
  Oxford University Press, 1942.

PINARD DE LA BOULLAYE, H., S.J. *Spiritual Exercises*. Paris:
  Beauchesne et ses fils, 1950.

PLE, ALBERT, O.P., ed. *Obedience*. Westminster, Maryland:
  The Newman Press, 1953.

POURRAT, PIERRE. *Christian Spirituality*. Vol. III. London: Burns
  Oates and Washbourne Ltd., 1927.

PURCELL, MARY. *The First Jesuit, St. Ignatius Loyola*. Westminster, Maryland: The Newman Press, 1957.

RAHNER, HUGO, S.J. *Notes on the Spiritual Exercises*, trans. by

Father Louis Mounteer. Woodstock: Woodstock College Press, 1956.

——————, *The Spirituality of St. Ignatius Loyola,* trans. by Francis John Smith, S.J. Westminster, Maryland: The Newman Press, 1953.

READ, HERBERT. *Form in Modern Poetry.* London: Sheed and Ward, 1932.

——————, "Poetry and Belief in Gerard Manley Hopkins," *New Verse* No. I, (Jan., 1933).

——————, "The Poetry of Gerard Manley Hopkins," *English Critical Essays, Twentieth Century.* London: Oxford University Press, 1933.

RICHARDS, I. A. *Practical Criticism.* London: Kegan Paul, 1935.

RUGGLES, ELEANOR. *Gerard Manley Hopkins. A Life.* New York: W. W. Norton and Co., 1944.

Summary of the Constitutions. Roehampton: Manresa Press, 1926.

THOMAS A KEMPIS. *The Following of Christ.* Edited by Rev. J. M. Lelen. New York: Catholic Book Publishing Co., 1941.

UNTERMEYER, LOUIS, ed. *Modern American and Modern British Poetry.* New York: Harcourt Brace, 1955.

VERMEERSCH, ARTHUR, S.J. *Meditations on the Summary of the Constitutions.* El Paso, Texas: Revista Catolica Press, 1951.

Victorian Poets, The: A Guide to Research. Ed. by Frederick E. Faverty. Cambridge, Mass.: Harvard University Press, 1956.

WAHNER, BERNARD F., S.J. "The Spiritual Exercises and the Ratio," *Jesuit Educational Quarterly,* XVI, No. 4, (March, 1954), 245-250.

WEYAND, NORMAN, S.J., ed. *Immortal Diamond: Studies in Gerard Manley Hopkins.* New York: Sheed and Ward, 1949.

WHITE, HELEN C. *English Devotional Literature, 1600-1640.* University of Wisconsin Studies in Language and Literature, No. 29. Madison: University of Wisconsin Press, 1931.

——————, *The Tudor Book of Private Devotion.* Madison: University of Wisconsin Press, 1951.

YOUNG, WILLIAM J., S.J. *The Ignatian Way to God,* trans. by Alexandre Brou, S.J. Milwaukee: The Bruce Publishing Company, 1952.

Index